EXPAND THE MIND

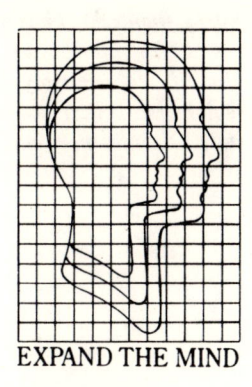

**ARTHUR
BORNSTEIN'S
MEMORY
TRAINING
COURSE**

Every man who knows how to read has it in his power to magnify himself, to multiply the ways in which he exists, to make his life full, significant and interesting.
—Aldous Huxley

Memory

Arthur Bornstein's Memory Training Course

Bornstein Memory Training Schools
West Los Angeles, California

Kendall/Hunt Publishing Company
Dubuque, Iowa

Copyright © 1964, 1979 by Arthur Bornstein

Seventh Printing, 1985

ISBN 0-8403-3745-0

All rights reserved. No part of this publication may be reproduced, stored in a retrieval system, or transmitted, in any form or by any means, electronic, mechanical, photocopying, recording, or otherwise, without the prior written permission of the copyright owner.

Printed in the United States of America

Arthur Bornstein

is the nation's leading authority on memory training methods.

Since 1952, when Mr. Bornstein founded his unique and highly successful School of Memory Training in Los Angeles, more than a million people from all walks of life and every corner of the world have trained their memories. Thousands of Memory Course graduates report how their lives have changed by achieving inner confidence, poise, and career advancement by applying his memory techniques.

Amazing feats of memory and skill in demonstrating and teaching his techniques have made Mr. Bornstein a celebrity in his own right. He has been invited to appear on every important radio and television show, with Johnny Carson, Steve Allen, Dinah Shore, Mike Douglas, the popular Bert Newton Show in Australia, and for fifteen years as a favorite guest speaker on Art Linkletter's television and radio programs.

Mr. Bornstein has become a favorite speaker and lecturer for business groups, college audiences, professional organizations, conventions, religious groups and civic clubs. He has conducted special memory training seminars and courses for many of the country's leading companies and business organizations, such as Hughes Aircraft, Lockheed, Carnation Co., and 20th Century-Fox.

Author of numerous articles in leading national magazines, he has been featured in hundreds of newspaper stories including Business Management, Teen, American Business, The Wall Street Journal, The Los Angeles Times, and Radio and Television Weekly.

He is responsible for many firsts in the field of memory training. Mr. Bornstein was the first person to introduce these techniques into the school system in California. Originator of the unique multiplication memorizer method for children, his system is currently used in more than 7,000 schools in the United States and Canada. As an educational consultant, he is recognized as a teacher of teachers.

A special commendation was presented to Mr. Bornstein by the California Legislature for his educational approach to memory training. His work as an educator has also been acknowledged by the fact that his courses and seminars are the first college-accredited memory training programs in the country. He and his staff teach special courses at UCLA, USC, Cal State Northridge, Orange Coast College, University of Hawaii, and many other colleges and universities.

His presentation has been heard from Hawaii to Greece and Australia to New York, by groups like the Young Presidents Organization, California Dental Association, Greater New York Dental Society, National Secretaries Association, American Institute of Banking. He is in demand to conduct executive development programs and as a national convention speaker.

He has also produced the first national television series on memory training, and his system was the basis of a special feature on the NBC television network for eleven million viewers of the Huntley-Brinkley evening newscast. Mr. Bornstein has also developed an audio cassette and video cassette course on memory training.

He has starred in a number of educational productions, including "Psychology Today's" film with David Steinberg and "As Man Behaves" with noted psychologist Matt Duncan. These are continually being shown on T.V. and at major universities, colleges and high schools throughout the world. Audiences find that Mr. Bornstein's presentation can literally be called unforgettable.

To

my students

and all the thinking people of the world

who wish to improve their minds

by improving their memories.

ACKNOWLEDGMENT

A Memory Training Course would indeed be incomplete without providing the reader with the maximum benefit of visual material to stimulate his mind and imagination. As Confucius said, "One picture is worth more than 10,000 words."

My sincere thanks, therefore, to D. L. Boyd and N. L. McMickle of Art Associates, Manhattan Beach, California, for the many fine illustrations used in this text. I feel these artists have the unique ability to project memory word ideas into stimulating and significant illustrations.

I wish to thank the many students who so graciously consented to having their photographs used for illustration and practice in the Names and Faces section. The many fine outstanding features of these individuals were captured by the expert photography of Bernard Bornstein and Bill Zigrang, to whom I am sincerely appreciative.

I am grateful to Eugene J. Maruca and Lorrie Foulks for their suggestions and many hours of research and editing assistance. Their interest and good humor, even in the small hours of the morning after fishburgers and many cups of coffee, made the writing of this memory course a pleasure for me.

FOREWORD

One night at a company dinner, an industrial relations director accurately introduced 160 people by their first and last names and company position without referring to notes. A number of those attending the meeting later admitted that they could not have introduced the half dozen co-workers at their own tables.

This remarkable feat of memory was a practical, although exaggerated, demonstration of techniques contained in this memory training course. They are techniques which once learned and practiced, can bring increased assurance and efficiency.

The unfailing ability to match names and faces is as important as it is rare. No other single attribute is as rewarding as the

R. S. BELL
Chairman of the Board
and President
Packard-Bell Electronics

ability to remember people by name. It might well be a business adage that "to remember is to be remembered."

An executive who can absorb copious data, sift it, evaluate it and bring pertinent details to mind at will is an invaluable asset to any company. His counterpart, who remembers only that the information exists somewhere in the files, can be replaced by a computer.

With just a little effort, the principles of memory training can be put to work by anyone. A student can attend lectures without taking notes. A business trainee can shorten his apprenticeship by learning faster. An executive can acquire the self-assurance that comes from knowing—and knowing that he knows.

Here are memory techniques as old as Aristotle, distilled into a compact course designed for today's fast-moving world.

Here is exciting adventure for all who take the time now to save time later—and for all who care to know what most educators fail to teach: how to learn and how to remember.

ROBERT S. BELL

PREFACE

> I have a son, Michael, 12 years of age, who is having a very hard time in school. It is about to drive me mad! I have tried different schools and taking him to doctors. His teachers and the doctors all say one thing—he is a bright child; there is not a thing wrong with him. He is of sound mind and health, but he just can't seem to learn. There is nothing more that I want in this world than to see my son get ahead.

A deeply concerned New Orleans mother wrote me this letter in desperation after seeing me on a national television show. In the same mail came another letter, this one from a 15-year-old Iowa girl. She wrote:

> The reason I'm writing is because no matter what I say or what I do it turns out to be a flop. (I guess I'm a failure.) I've got everything a girl could possibly want. I'm sure there is no mental disorder. The thing I really fear is my grades in school—there will be a lot of memorization which will be murder for me. PLEASE try to help me.

This worried mother, the distraught student, brought back memories of my own frustrating days as a struggling student at the University of Miami.

I remember well how, night after night, I would study endlessly, repeating my text material over and over and over, for hours on end. I had no systematic approach. I was never taught a systematic approach to make vast quantities of new information stick in my mind.

At examination time I would think that my studies would be thoroughly assimilated after all the repetition. But I found, when I would try to write down the answers I thought I knew so well, the blank paper would stare up at me and my mind was as blank as that paper! The sick feeling of mounting anxiety and tension was awful, along with that frustrating mental block!

My friends, who took the same courses with me, from the same instructors, would be asleep at eleven P.M. I would still be grinding away at the same textbooks and class notes at two in the morning. I couldn't understand why my friends would get A's and B's when I, who worked so hard, barely passed with C's and D's.

I was worried! My professors told me that I was not college material. The dean even told me, "You don't belong in college. Your father is in business. Perhaps you should go into business with him."

But I wanted a college education! I wouldn't give up, and after a conference with the dean, I persuaded him to let me stay another semester. He agreed to put me on probation, provided I could make B's and C's during the next semester. I promised myself that I would somehow find a way to make these grades.

That entire evening I spent walking up and down in my room. I asked myself, "What's wrong with me? Think of the hours wasted reading and rereading only to have the material slip my mind when it really counted! The secret of good grades is a good memory, and I can't remember what I study long enough to put it down on the exam paper!" My mind repeated these thoughts over and over again and they have proven true.

For three days and nights this thought plagued me, MEMORY! MEMORY! How can I learn to remember what I study? I wondered if I was born with a bad memory and decided I wasn't. My memory was good enough for some things.

I looked casually around the room and began to consider: "If I had to remember every item in this room how would I go about doing it?"

I looked at my tennis racket, the mirror on the wall above it, and my history book. How would I remember these three items? There must be a way to impress them on my mind! I stared at the tennis racket and the mirror and said, "I've got to see them going together."

The picture came to me of the tennis racket hitting the mirror. But the mirror and book had no logical connection, so I used my imagination to see that book pasted on the mirror. I looked away, and again I thought of the tennis racket. This time I found a complete picture in my mind of all *three* items coming together as if they were one thought.

But, that's only three items! I thought, what if I had to remember ten? So I decided to try. I glanced around the room and saw my radio, the window, a pennant, pillow, socks, T-shirt and pen.

Continuing from the book, I saw it falling onto the radio. Then I saw the radio on the window sill. I looked at the pennant and saw it hanging on the window. Then I wrapped the pennant around the pillow. Next I saw the socks—pillow and socks? They really don't belong together but I decided I would *make* them go together. I pictured the pillow being stuffed into my socks. It was a ridiculous picture but I thought I'd try it anyway.

PREFACE *xiii*

My socks and T-shirt—I saw my socks tied around my T-shirt. Then I looked at my pen and hung this pen onto my T-shirt.

I wondered, could I remember these 10 items? To test myself I walked out of my room into the hall. I thought of the tennis racket . . . immediately the mirror came to mind, then the book . . . it fell on the radio . . . the radio was on the window sill. Hanging onto the window was the pennant, which suddenly became wrapped around the pillow. The pillow was being stuffed into my socks. Then I could still see the socks tied around my T-shirt with the pen hanging from it.

I became excited as I recalled all 10 items one right after the other! They came back rapidly! Happily I asked, "Am I the fellow who can't remember? Why, that was easy!"

I was so excited that I ran into the next room where my good friend, Bert Baxt, was studying. With enthusiasm in my voice, I told him of my startling discovery. He looked at me quizzically as I related my experience. I said, "Bert, you try it, and see if my new way to remember works for you!"

I showed him how I had remembered the 10 items in my room, and to his amazement he also remembered the list.

This was the beginning of my adventures in memory miracles.

A.B.

CONTENTS

FOREWORD BY R. S. BELL, ix

PREFACE, xi

ONE: THE VALUE OF A GOOD MEMORY, 1
    What You Will Accomplish from This Memory Course, 3   Success in Every Field Can Be Traced to a Good Memory, 5

TWO: THE MEMORY YOU WERE BORN WITH, 9
    Your Five Senses and Your Memory, 10   Find Out Which Sense Aids Your Memory Most, 12   Test Your Eye Memory, 13   Test Your Ear Memory, 14   Test Your Motor Memory, 15   How You Remember Through the Laws of Logical Association, 17   Apply Laws of Logical Association, 25

THREE: MEMORY SYSTEMS, 29
    Five Systems, 32   I. Cue Systems, 32   II. Visual Key Systems, 35   III. Initial System of Remembering, 37   IV. Cues Using Logic and Imagination, 38   V. Observation and Association, 40

FOUR: LET'S LEARN A SYSTEM, 43
    Complete Numerical Alphabet, 51

FIVE: HOW TO APPLY THE SYSTEM, 61

SIX: REMEMBER ISOLATED FACTS, 83
    Bring Home the Groceries, 84   Communicate with Others, 85   Where Did I Park My Car? 85   Looking for Your Pen, 86   Jog Your Memory, 86   Locked Out! 87   Do I Have Everything? 87   Forget-Me-Not, 88   Where Is My Car? 88   Have a Place for Everything, 88   Review Chart of 100 Visual Key Words, 92

CONTENTS xv

SEVEN: HOW TO REMEMBER NAMES AND FACES, 93
  The Six Easy Steps, 96 **Find the Features,** 102 **Ten Techniques for Associating Names,** 104 **Use Your Imagination to Associate,** 107 **Meet Six People,** 109 **Additional Practice in Association,** 115

EIGHT: REMEMBER FIRST NAMES
  AND FACTS ABOUT PEOPLE, 117
  Remember Facts About People, 123 **Use Your Imagination: Project Your Associations,** 127 **How to Meet Large Groups of People,** 131 **Final Review,** 132 **Review Steps to Remembering Names and Faces,** 137

NINE: CONCENTRATE, OBSERVE AND CLASSIFY, 139
  I. It Pays to Observe, 139 **II. Learn How to Concentrate!** 144 **III. Classification: An Aid to Memory,** 146

TEN: HOW TO REMEMBER TELEPHONE NUMBERS, 153
  Memorize the Telephone Area Codes, 157 **Extension Numbers: Apply the Same Technique,** 161 **Street Addresses,** 161 **Remember Telephone Numbers,** 162 **Exchanges and Exchange Numbers,** 162 **All Number Dialing,** 164 **Telephone Number Record,** 171

ELEVEN: THE CUE METHOD OF MEMORIZING, 173

TWELVE: A FOREIGN LANGUAGE IN HALF THE TIME! 187
  Increase Your Spanish Vocabulary, 188 **A New Way to Learn Spanish,** 190 **Let's Learn French,** 193 **Let's Learn German,** 195

THIRTEEN: LET'S TEST YOUR MEMORY POWER, 199
  Remember the Presidents, 200 **Memorize the Presidents in Numerical Order,** 203 **Presidents and Year They Entered Office,** 210 **How to Remember Historical Dates,** 213 **Memorize the State Capitals,** 216 **Remember World Capitals,** 221

FOURTEEN: ADDITIONAL PRACTICAL APPLICATION, 223
How to Increase Your Vocabulary, 223   **How to Improve Your Spelling,** 225   **Remember Stock Symbols,** 230   **Important Atomic Elements,** 232   **Be an Optimist!** 234   **Memorize the Cues in Sequence,** 237   **Write It Verbatim,** 238   **Verbatim Learning Techniques,** 239

THE VALUE OF A GOOD MEMORY

Chapter One

"The first thing an executive must have is a fine memory. Of course, it does not follow that the man with a fine memory is necessarily a fine executive. But if he has the memory, he has the first qualification. And if he has not the memory, nothing else matters!"
—Thomas Alva Edison

Consider these thought-provoking words of Thomas Edison, and apply them to well known and successful persons. Fame and millions of dollars have been acquired by individuals who have applied a good memory towards specific goals.

In cases of outstanding success in

virtually every field, the individual's retentive mind has played a dominant role in attaining his ultimate goal. Some such men and women who have achieved international recognition are General Alfred Gruenther, Daniel Webster, Elsa Maxwell, James Farley, General George C. Marshall, Charles Evans Hughes, Arturo Toscanini, Sir Winston Churchill, Amy Vanderbilt, the former Dean of Harvard Law School, Roscoe Pound, real estate developer William Zeckendorf, General Douglas MacArthur, and Norman Vincent Peale. The leadership of these people has ranged into every field from government to music, from the army to society, from industry to party-giving and from law to religion.

Talents vary, interests are often far apart. Educational background and way of living frequently are in great contrast. However, these world renowned individuals have been noted for one thing in common: a good memory. Like virtually every successful man or woman, they have used their ability to remember to the greatest advantage!

It is a common misconception that as you grow older, your memory grows weaker. The older you get, the better your memory should become. Your mind stores information by classifying and associating new ideas with ideas which you already possess. You should have a better memory at the age of 50 than at the age of 18. Winston Churchill, Herbert Hoover and Bernard McFadden, when in their seventies and eighties, had minds as keen as when they were 30 years younger.

Most people, whether young or old, who claim to have a poor memory usually are individuals who have not exercised their memories. They have lost interest and confidence in their ability to learn and to remember.

Thomas De Quincey said, "The memory strengthens as you lay burdens on it, and becomes trustworthy as you trust it."

A classic example of a man who has applied his memory to great advantage is General Alfred Gruenther. *Time* magazine, in its February 6, 1956 issue, related this interesting background of General Gruenther:

> He took a memory course when he was 13 . . . NATO's indispensable man has been described as a human IBM machine, the perfect staff officer, the smartest man in the U.S. Army, the most factual man of his time.
>
> Mindful of his mission, Gruenther lets no group that might influence opinion pass through Paris unnoticed. Whatever the group, he whips off a Gruenthergram demanding information. (I should like to know more about the Machine Tool Association whom we are briefing on Friday. What are some of their problems?) By the time he has to

speak, he knows that the group comprises 29 manufacturers from eight countries, is highly interested in developing and adopting standardized equipment for NATO needs, and that he can warmly commend them on their interest. With such a preface, he swings into his discussion of the structure and importance of NATO, reeling off statistics without recourse to notes, as usual.

While Chief of NATO, General Gruenther was invited to Parliament. He knew he would be reviewing 120 Military Police honor guards. He had his aides get photographs of each soldier and provide short biographies about each one. The night before, he scanned each photograph and memorized facts about each soldier. The next morning he walked down the ranks, called each soldier by name, spoke with him briefly and commented, "How's your wife, Mary?" "How's your new daughter?" "How's the weather in Boston?" There was a look of amazement on each soldier's face. Here was a general who took time to remember the ordinary soldier by name.

General Gruenther began life with the same ability to remember as the rest of us. By applying memory training techniques over the years, his mind has become a natural storehouse of information.

I know that by mastering and *using* the memory techniques presented in this course you too can develop your memory to the highest level possible.

What You Will Accomplish from This Memory Course

In this course, you will learn how to use your powers of concentration, association, visualization, imagination and classification to remember all types of material. You will see how important these *natural* abilities are for retaining names and faces, numbers, text material, vocabulary, foreign languages, historical and geographical data—anything you may need to remember.

This course is designed with exercises to strengthen your memory in all areas. You will be taught effective memory methods to remember names and faces as well as memorizing foreign words or increasing your English vocabulary. You will apply related methods to remember how to spell and to memorize telephone numbers.

Keep in mind that the more you apply and practice the memory exercises in this course, the stronger your ability will become in all memory areas. Strength comes with exercise. Just as muscles weaken with disuse so will the memory patterns of the mind weaken with disuse.

You might compare yourself to a baseball player going into spring training before the big season begins. He would not expect to be in top condition in two weeks. It will require more like two months of training. This training period conditions his body and sharpens his physical and mental reflexes. After this period of training, he would be able to think quickly, to hit, catch and throw the ball with speed and accuracy.

You are going into your memory training camp to learn various methods and techniques for memory retention. You will condition your mind to be in complete control of memory situations you may encounter now or in the future. Remember, your memory will strengthen as you practice the many exercises in this course. In a few days you will notice great improvement. After two months of continual application of the prescribed methods your mind will know when and how to control a memory challenge and have immediate recall as well as lasting retention for that particular subject.

Most people do not apply enough imagination to their everyday lives. In this course, you will learn to use your imagination actively. It will be stressed continually. You will also use logic when obvious relationships can be seen. Individuals differ. You might apply more logic whereas another person would emphasize more imagination. My approach to memory training is very direct. Use the techniques that work best for you, but you should know and practice all the techniques presented.

The methods I use cover a wide range of material. As you practice and apply the exercises in this course, you will find your thought processes getting sharper and sharper; vivid mental pictures will come to mind more and more rapidly; strong concrete associations will be made with assurance. You will find constant use for application in your chosen field. Demonstrations to your friends of your newly acquired controlled memory methods will bring confidence and pleasure to you, not only for the moments of application, but throughout your entire life. You can be the master of any memory situation.

Rote memory—that is, repeatedly going over material until it is learned— will be replaced by a systematic approach to acquiring knowledge so that it will come back to mind when you need it. Promise yourself that you will practice each exercise prescribed in this course. Discipline your mind to accept these new methods. Apply these principles to all memory situations in the future.

Whether you are a student, businessman, executive, housewife, artist or professional man or woman, you must break away from your old patterns of learning. Let your mind accept my systematic approach to learning. You may already use some good techniques that help you to remember. For example, you may have a system of putting your car keys on top of your wallet every evening so that you don't spend time looking for them the next morning. Keep using these good techniques, but add new methods to help you learn and remember more.

Success in Every Field Can Be Traced to a Good Memory

Your knowledge is of little value unless you have it at your fingertips at the right time.

The doctor's observation must be keen and thorough. They must recall whether this is the same type of symptom he or she has seen before, even if it was five days, five weeks, or five years ago. One characteristic which is slightly different could change the diagnosis. Memory can make the difference between the right or wrong decision. By demonstrating knowledge through the faculty called memory, individuals can become the leading expert in their field.

The housewife can't look in her notebook when she meets her new neighbor in the supermarket. She can only say, "Hello there, Mrs. Er-Mmmm."

The businessperson at a conference will highlight the meeting by bringing forth more facts and information than anyone else present.

Students realize the importance of memory at examination time. They cannot tell their teacher that they knew all the material the night before. They must perform NOW, and the only proof that they have the needed knowledge is through the use of memory. Memory is actually the storehouse of knowledge.

Any professional person will realize greater success in his or her chosen career because, as the expert in the field, he will gain more clients and prestige as a result of the ability to remember at the right time!

When Chief Justice Charles Evans Hughes was still practicing law, he would make it a point to quote in court page after page of case precedents having a bearing on the case he was pleading. While other lawyers were forced to read such references from books or typed notes, Mr. Hughes reeled them off verbatim and solely from memory.

The expert lawyer who can remember courtroom and deposition testimony, case precedents, jurors' names and all pertinent data, stands out above all colleagues and leaves an indelible impression on the judge, jury, clients and witnesses. He stands out as the expert. Obviously they know more about the case and related law than anyone else in the courtroom!

The salesperson who remembers sales points earns more commissions. He or she cannot make the right impression if forced to say that the information is back at the office. The customer wants to know about the merchandise right now! The salesperson who has the information at his fingertips instead of in the file at the office will be the one most likely to make the sale.

An excellent example of the tangible value of a good memory to a salesperson is an experience that one of my students, Leon Ungar, of Ungar Sales Associates, related to me after he had returned from a national electronics convention in New Orleans.

Buyers from all over the country were assembled at this convention in the late summer for the purpose of hearing about many manufacturers' products. Orders were not usually given during this convention, but were decided upon and placed after the buyers returned to their respective cities and stores.

Leon was scheduled as the last speaker of the day. It was an extremely hot afternoon, and he knew that all the men would be tired and anxiously awaiting the end of the day. Leon kept thinking, "How can I gain their attention and make them listen to me tell about our products?" In the taxi on the way to the meeting Leon suddenly recalled what I had told him in our session on remembering names, faces and facts about people: "Everyone pays attention to what you have to say if you call them by name first."

So he decided to try something unique at this convention. He had a list of buyers' names, department stores and cities from which they came. He stopped at an out-of-town newsstand and bought papers from cities represented by the buyers. He proceeded to memorize the names of the buyers, the name of the store each represented and the city in which it was located. Scanning the newspapers he had bought, he also memorized some facts about each city, such as the weather, baseball scores, etc.

When it was his turn to talk about his products, he was ready! For the first 10 minutes of his allotted 30-minute time period, he called each man by name and mentioned the store he represented. Then he gave each man the weather report from his city or the local baseball score.

By the time he began his sales presentation, all the men were sitting on the edge of their seats in fascination, paying close attention to what he had to say. When he had completed his presentation, they rushed up with congratulations. That night and the next day, they sought him out with order

THE VALUE OF A GOOD MEMORY

books in hand. He returned to Los Angeles with $15,000 in orders. Even at subsequent conventions years afterwards, some men still comment on his feat of memory with amazement. Everyone remembers Leon!

Another of my students who has achieved signal success through applying my memory training methods to his work is Jack Beyerlein.

When Jack took my course he had just started a new job with A. Cohen and Son, the largest wholesale jewelers in the world. His work included sales supervision, purchasing, credit and management.

Jack applied all the many phases of memory training to his job—and he must have done it well. He learned the prices and style numbers of literally thousands of items, as well as the names and addresses of the manufacturers and distributors of about 4,000 different items. At the same time he had to give answers, and quickly, to a crew of salesmen covering the 11 western states. He did a tremendous job!

The West Coast Branch Manager of A. Cohen and Son had held his position for 19 years when he passed away unexpectedly. The executives of the firm flew out from the East to select his successor.

Many of the men in line for this vacant position had been with the company for years, while Jack had joined the firm only five months before. Yet he knew so much more about the entire organization and all its products than any of these men that no one but Jack could be chosen for the job! He was selected as manager of the entire West Coast operations, with a 50 per cent increase in salary!

Today he is Vice-President of Leroy's Jewelers in Los Angeles. When he left A. Cohen and Son, his work had to be split up among *three* men. Jack told me recently, when he invited me for a week-end trip, "Art, thanks to you and your fabulous course, I have a 35-foot cabin cruiser!"

Everyone would like to be an expert in his or her field. Each person can be an expert. For, after all, the expert is the person who knows more about a given subject, whether it be about his company or product or profession. They are experts because they can remember more than anyone else at the right time!

This course will condition your mind to visualize ideas to the highest possible degree. Remember, the more you put into this course, the more you will get out of it. Keep in mind the analogy of the baseball player training for the big season. If the techniques are developed correctly, then you will achieve the desired results.

At my school, in my classes for industry and through my television and radio courses, I have trained thousands of students to use their minds more effectively.

So many of my students have doubled and tripled their earning capacities by applying these techniques that I do not have the available space to tell you of all of them. Students have cut study time in half, and some have raised their grades from failing to honor roll in one semester's time. Housewives have become confident by proving to their husbands and children that they, individually, have a keen mind and the ability to remember.

Individual students will acquire different results. You may become a more confident person, become an expert at remembering names and faces, or you may learn how to relax. You may get a better job, or just make a lifetime hobby of learning foreign languages quickly. You will most certainly enjoy this new memory power which you possess.

Look for application in your everyday life. Remember to put to use the methods you are learning—names, faces, numbers, vocabulary, spelling, or just practice by remembering a list of 50 items to amaze your friends.

Make what you learn become a permanent part of your thinking ability. You will gain rich rewards for the rest of your life!

THE MEMORY YOU WERE BORN WITH

Chapter **Two**

The noblest tool of every person is the mind, and its value is determined by the use he or she makes of it. This tool is a gift endowed by nature.

The native memory begins to function at a very early age. An infant recognizes people through sight and sound; remembers objects through touch, and food through taste and smell. As the infant matures, the more he or she will experience through these natural faculties, the better the basis will be developed for the retention of new knowledge.

This chapter is primarily concerned with eye, ear and motor (touch) senses. These are the basic senses used in learning. As you go through the exercises in this memory course, you may notice that material you read or see will return to mind rapidly. If so, you have a predominantly "eye-memory." If you notice that speaking aloud helps you to remember something, then you have a predominantly "ear-memory." On the other hand, if you remember what you write more effectively, then write your associations out, thus bringing the motor sense into active part in making the impression.

Your Five Senses and Your Memory

1. Memory Through Sight

Most people are predominantly eye minded; that is, they remember what they see more than what they hear. The reason for this is that we use our eyes continually throughout each day. It is an over-developed sense for most individuals. In contrast, a blind person's sense of hearing and touch is developed to an extremely high degree because of continual use. He doesn't have the actual visual sense with which to remember; therefore, he compensates by over-development of the other two.

Let's test your visual sense of remembering.

Think of your kitchen. Visualize the sink—notice that your mind will go to the location. Now picture the stove. Visualize the silverware drawer open . . . focus your attention on the spoons . . . now the forks and knives.

Now switch the picture to a lake scene, with racing boats.

Switch your picture again to that of a playground scene, with children laughing and running, sliding on the board, and swinging on the swings.

If you are visual minded, you will notice that your mind will automatically change your mental picture. You as an individual may see a more vivid picture than the next person simply because you have observed more detail of that particular item, place or person.

Referring back to your scene of the kitchen, a Navy man's concept would vary from a housewife's. His "kitchen" would be a galley with huge kettles and stainless steel sinks. His silverware would have the imprint U.S.N. Even twenty years after he has left the service, he would still hold a lasting visual impression of the initials U.S.N. on this silverware.

If your motive and interest is directed toward photography and you are very familiar with different types of cameras, the word "Speedgraphic" will bring a vivid picture to mind of a particular camera. The person without some technical knowledge of photography or cameras will not react to the word "Speedgraphic."

The closer you observe, the keener your attention to detail, the stronger the impression on your visual memory.

2. Memory Through Hearing

Let's suppose that you went by a fire house and the bell rang at that moment. The memory of the sound of the bell and the association with that sound makes us have an emotional reaction when we hear it again. If you had never heard the sound of a fire bell, there would be no reaction from you.

Reproduce the sound of a bell in your mind as you read this—try it! Dwell upon the sound of ringing bells for 10 seconds. Did you hear them? Now think of a dog barking: first the thought then the reproduction of the sound. This is a relatively simple example of your auditory memory working.

The person with a highly developed auditory sense can accurately reproduce words, numbers, phrases or expression of ideas which he has heard. Oral communication can register a strong impact. This can include the phraseology and even the intonation of the speaker's voice.

That is why the person with an acute auditory sense remembers more from hearing a lecture than reading a book. He can actually reproduce the words he has heard at a future time, thereby giving him more lasting retention of the spoken word.

3. Memory Through Touch (Motor)

Your motor memory is the retracing of a pattern that you have experienced through your sense of touch. Take this page and run your fingers over it. Imagine that you are touching, not paper, but *velvet*. Feel it, notice the tingling sensation in the tips of your fingers. This sensation is created because your fingertips relay to the memory the actual feel of velvet. A child who has never touched a piece of velvet would not experience this sensation.

You may have experienced writing a telephone number on a note pad in your office. Later in the day, while at home, when you need the number you can think back and recreate the feeling of writing this number. You can write or recite it again because of your motor memory. After you have dialed this number several times, your motor memory may take over so that the next time you wish to dial the same number, your fingers automatically move to the positions on the dial.

The person possessing a highly developed motor sense can easily reproduce what he has written. He mentally retraces the patterns that he has experienced through his fingers.

*4. and 5. Memory Through Taste
and Smell*

Little explanation is needed for these senses. They recall the pleasant or unpleasant experiences you have had with both smell and taste from early childhood.

Think of steak and onions sizzling on a grill . . . smell it . . . now taste it . . . you may also notice your mouth is watering.

In contrast to the pleasant experiences, you would not drink vinegar straight from the bottle because your sense of taste will remember and flash the message to your mind that vinegar tastes sour. These are automatic reactions within your mind.

In this memory training course, you will notice that more emphasis is placed on the senses of sight, hearing and touch, because these senses aid your memory in retaining facts and ideas to a greater degree than do your senses of taste or smell.

Find Out Which Sense Aids Your Memory Most

Of the three main "memory senses" you will find that one sense is more productive than the other two for recall. However, all three main senses—eye, ear and motor—tend to support each other.

As an example, you call *Information* for a telephone number. When she gives it to you, your auditory sense comes into play. When you write it down, your motor sense is used. When you see it written down, you are using your visual sense. So when you are exposed to the number, all three senses are actually used and they work together to help you.

You will notice that in the chapter on remembering names and faces, all three senses will be employed:

Visual—when you observe the face and outstanding features.

Auditory—when you repeat the name.
Motor—when you write down the person's name.

If you sketch a person's facial characteristics, you would use all three senses:

Motor—when you draw the sketch.
Visual—as you picture or recall the features.
Auditory—as you say the person's name.

You can get an indication of whether your eye, ear or motor sense best helps you remember by taking the three survey exercises which follow. Each exercise consists of a story containing at least 20 facts. The story from which you remember the most facts will indicate whether your eye, ear or motor memory brings forth the greatest recall. Recognizing this will help you realize which sense aids your memory the most.

Keep in mind when evaluating these ear, eye and motor survey exercises that you may have an advantage because of past experiences, such as being familiar with a certain scene, or incident or term.

Test Your Eye Memory

Read the following story just once. Write what you remember on a separate sheet of paper after only *one* reading. Then compare your list of facts with the story below.

> Mr. Perkins, a retired postal clerk, was driving his red station wagon down Orange Grove Avenue. The light suddenly turned red. A sick feeling came over him as his foot hit the brake and his car kept going. Seeing other cars starting to cross his path he turned to avoid a collision and his car screeched to the right.
>
> He managed to avoid the seven pedestrians waiting for the bus, but before he could bring his car out of the sharp turn, it jumped the curb and struck the bright yellow fire hydrant about ten feet from the intersection.
>
> As water gushed to second story height, people came from everywhere. There must have been more than 150 of them milling around.
>
> A young rookie policeman directing traffic ran to his call box located on the opposite corner to summon aid. Seven minutes later, police cars and fire trucks arrived. The water was shut off and the crowd dispersed.

Mr. Perkins was given a citation for faulty brakes and a notice to appear in Judge Blake's Court at 10:30 a.m. the next Thursday. Mr. Perkins surveyed the scene with complete disgust. The final dejection came when the man with the tow truck said, "Where do you want your car towed to, Buddy?"

Number of Facts Recalled Correctly _____

Test Your Ear Memory

Ask someone to read this story to you just once. As you recite the facts, have the other person compare them to the story below. Or write what you remember on a separate sheet of paper, then compare the facts with the story again.

Prices opened mixed on the New York Stock Exchange this morning, but by noon an upward trend in the popular averages had been established. Blue chip stocks gained almost a point or more.

This strength may carry over to tomorrow's market but a testing may likely occur sometime next week.

The Dow Jones Averages list Industrials up 4.69; Railroads up .70; Utilities up 1.13. Volume was 2,350,000 shares.

So went the endless ticker tape and bulletins as youthful Gary Phillips donned his coat to leave for lunch at Joey's Counter down the street. Now for another chance to review his Philosophy. Gary loved Philosophy. It made sense to him. Eating and thinking always revitalized him. After ordering his usual lunch, he pulled some notes from his pocket and mused over them.

ARISTOTLE: He sought to find cause-and-effect relationships in the world by using the Laws of Logic. He made valuable contributions to deductive and inductive logic.

IMMANUEL KANT: We get impressions through our senses but our minds shape and organize these impressions until they become meaningful. He believed that opinion is a judgment insufficiently based, subjectively as well as objectively.

JOHN LOCKE: The mind is a blank tablet upon which experience writes. Knowledge is simply the connection and separation of ideas.

It was now 12:40. Walking unhurriedly back to the office, Gary

THE MEMORY YOU WERE BORN WITH 15

thought, 45 minutes is a short time for eating and thinking. The office seemed quieter now and as he sat down at his desk the latest bulletin was coming in.

"638 stocks advanced . . . 320 declined . . . 232 unchanged . . ."

NUMBER OF FACTS RECALLED CORRECTLY _____

Test Your Motor Memory

Your motor memory is working when you can experience tracing a pattern with your fingers and then recreate that experience again correctly. The following is a reproduction of a telephone dial. With your forefinger, trace this series of numbers, one at a time, as though you were dialing them on a telephone:

9 7 0 4 8 6 2 1 8 3 9 1 3 6 4

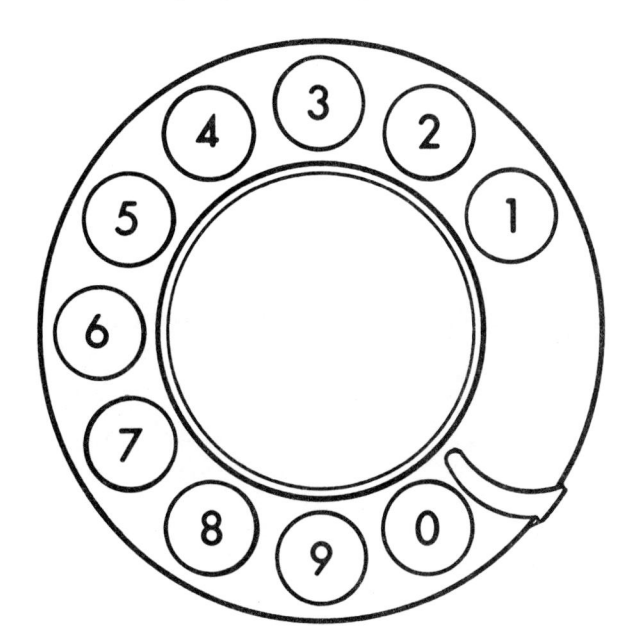

Now, try to retrace the numbers you have just "dialed" once again. As you do, write the numbers on the lines below. If you have a strong motor memory, you should be able to trace the correct numbers in their original sequence. Compare your numbers with the original series.

16   THE MEMORY YOU WERE BORN WITH

___ ___ ___ ___ ___ ___ ___ ___

___ ___ ___ ___ ___ ___ ___

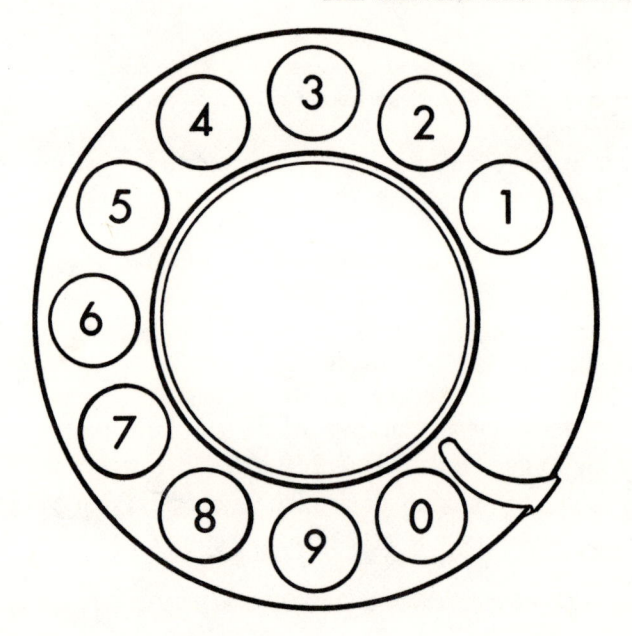

AMOUNT OF NUMBERS RECALLED CORRECTLY _____

Note: The three preceding exercises should not be construed to be actual psychological tests. They are intended to give you a more thorough understanding of how your eye, ear and motor senses are used to help you remember. The exercises in this memory training course are designed to develop these memory senses to the highest level possible. Since every person has a certain degree of eye, ear and motor memory, the objective here is to become as skilled as possible in using all three. The two senses which may not be as fully developed as the third can be strengthened with continued practice and conditioning.

Having discussed the way in which the five senses serve your memory, now let us see how your mind will associate material in a logical pattern.

We can remember things which seem to go together naturally because our subconscious mind automatically associates them. These fundamental relationships will be referred to as the *Laws of Logical Association*.

This basic process of logical association is based upon four classifications:

1. Similarity
2. Contrast
3. Contiguity
4. Whole and Part

How You Remember Through the Laws of Logical Association

1. Retention Through Similarity

A. *SIGHT*—You possess thousands of mental pictures in your conscious and subconscious mind. You will see how these mental pictures will enable you to link new information to these stored impressions. You meet someone—he is wearing a mustache—who reminds you of your Uncle Henry—yet you may not have seen your Uncle Henry in ten years. The thought that runs through your mind is—Uncle Henry has a mustache similar to Mr. Jones', the man you have just met.

When you drive by the house where you lived in the past, thoughts of the neighbors run through your mind. If I say "picture the grade school you attended when you were ten years old," different people will get different pictures.

You always remember the object, or the person, the way he looked the last time you were exposed to the impression. Assume you went back to your home town and found that your old grade school had been torn down and a new one built in its place. Viewing the new structure, then you would have two mental images in mind, the old and the new.

In the memory course, you will use this basic law to a very high degree. All of your past experience and knowledge will be used to tie new information into your memory. The more you observe and experience, the more mental images you will have in your subconscious mind. They will be utilized as basic associations to hold new ideas in place. There are constant visual reminders in your everyday life that serve as springboards to bring old and new associations to mind.

B. *SOUND*—Association through sound, such as words that sound similar, aids your memory. The average child and adult has thousands of sound associations ready made. As an example, when I say the word "ball," you should be able to sound out at least ten other words that have similar sounds, such as fall, call, all, gall, hall, haul, tall, maul, Paul, pall, Saul, wall, yawl. If you were trying to think of a place in South America that sounds like Equator, then Ecuador would come to mind, or Pakistan sounds like "pack on a stand." Notice the illustration—even an abstract word like *because* sounds like "bee" and "gauze."

If you tried to think of the name of the 30th President, and you had an idea that it sounded something like cool—cool ledge—through the sounds of cool and ledge, Coolidge would come to mind.

These words are recalled through the similarity of sounds. Children as well as adults will make strong associations by using both sound and sight associations. They will be used often in our course because these particular faculties are the two most highly developed and actively used by most individuals.

C. *SYNONYMS*—Synonyms are words that have a similar meaning but are not spelled alike. Synonyms help us recall words that mean the same thing.

In conversation, if you cannot think of a certain word to express an idea you can choose another to say the same thing. When speaking, you wouldn't intentionally be repetitious. You quickly think of another word or phrase that means the same and expresses the same idea.

Have you ever written an examination paper, and found that you couldn't spell a particular word? You thought for a moment and then came up with a word you *could* spell and had the same meaning.

You are having a conversation about a car. You say, "That's a good looking car." Another person says, "How much did the vehicle cost?" The third person says, "Could I take a drive in the automobile?" All of you are talking about the same thing but three different words are used.

Think of the word big, then think again: the word large comes to mind, then huge, extreme, gigantic, etc. In short, synonyms aid the memory because they act as a classification of words and ideas to be drawn upon at will to aid in the expression of ideas.

D. *SPECIES AND SORT*—This is a general law of classification of over-all ideas. When you think of transportation, thoughts of the kinds of transportation should run through your mind: auto, train, bus, ships, bicycle, etc.

If on the other hand you thought of a piece of chalk, you could trace it back to its species, which would be writing implements.

When recalling a fact about a person, you may think of the economic classification first, such as: he works for a grocery chain, or he is a butcher, or he works for a department store, or I know he sells furniture.

2. Retention Through Contrast

This law is somewhat self-explanatory; things that are opposite tend to come to mind automatically. Big—little. Hot—cold. New—old. Far—near. Hard—soft. Excellent—poor. Good—bad, etc. Associations through contrast may be made when remembering an individual's name such as Mr. Long, who is a short man, or Mr. Stern, who is a man with a very kind voice and face.

3. Retention Through Contiguity

Let's first define the word *contiguity*. It means items or events that run in a series or that are next to, or near, in time and place. The following headings will give a more thorough understanding of the Law of Contiguity.

A. *CAUSE AND EFFECT*—A cause and effect relationship is the result of an action that produces a reaction. This reaction may affect a person, place or thing. In chemistry, we know that if we mix two chemicals we will have an effect. In everyday cooking, you put a pot of water on the stove. The flame under the pot causes the water to boil. Drop two eggs in the water, and in five minutes, the effect—hard boiled eggs.

So your everyday life is affected to a high degree by this one basic law. As an example: A man has a great compulsion for smoking. One Monday evening at 11:55 P.M. he realizes he is completely out of cigarettes. He dashes from the house to his automobile. He has seven blocks to drive and the store closes at 12:00 midnight. He stops at a red light, looks both ways, sees no cars coming so he proceeds. A moment later, he sees flashing red lights behind him, and an officer writes him a ticket. He doesn't get his cigarettes that evening, but three days later is downtown at the traffic court to pay his fine. While walking back to his car, he slips on a banana peel, injures his hip, is out of work for three weeks. A constant fight with his wife ensues because of this, and they are now thinking of a divorce. Why? It all can be traced back to that Monday night when he left his house to buy cigarettes.

In the field of medicine, this cause and effect relationship is ever-present. You go to the doctor with a pain, which is usually the effect. The doctor determines the cause of this pain and then takes the necessary steps to eliminate the pain.

Cause and effect is applied by recognizing a tracing action between one thought and another. What happens tomorrow is dependent upon what happens today. If you want to think back and remember where you placed a certain item, such as a book, you would use cause and effect in reverse to determine the location: where was I when I put the book down, did I have it yesterday? In other words, retrace your steps.

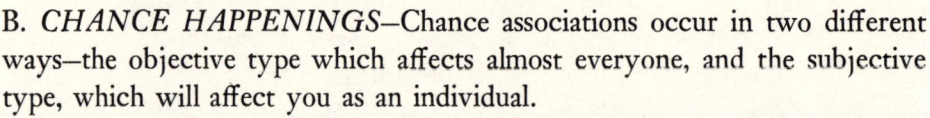

B. *CHANCE HAPPENINGS*—Chance associations occur in two different ways—the objective type which affects almost everyone, and the subjective type, which will affect you as an individual.

As an example of the objective type of association, if I said 1492, your reaction would be, that was the year Columbus discovered America. This date was established in our memories to represent a fact. If Columbus had been delayed on his voyage, then it could have been 1497 that we would remember and not 1492. The fact that Columbus discovered America in 1492 was something that happened by CHANCE, because it could have happened at any other time.

In your own life your subjective experiences create strong mental impressions. These impressions enable you to associate new ideas in the future. As an example, suppose you were standing on a street corner and suddenly two cars collided. Your name was taken as a witness. At the time you were quite upset, seeing the accident, the officer's questions, etc. Months go by and you hear nothing about the accident.

One year later you go by that same street corner for the first time since the accident. What thought will come to your mind? Correct! The thought of the accident. Yet thousands of people go by that same corner and have no thought of the accident. You, as an individual, having been at this place at that particular time *by chance*, now have the definite association in mind.

Use places you are familiar with as symbols for associating new facts. Meet me on the street corner where that fire happened two weeks ago. An object such as a camera, wristwatch or ring, for instance, can be used to symbolize an experience, event or place.

All of your past experiences—people you have met, places you have visited—can be used to hold onto new ideas. You meet a man who attended the same high school your cousin attended. This becomes a subjective association. You will remember the school the man attended because you now have an association. This man and your cousin. If you want to think of the name of the school this man attended, then think of your cousin.

C. *COMBINATIONS*—Things we expect to go together, such as names, objects and places, naturally are recalled together. When you think of ham— eggs come to mind. Pen—pencil. Shoes—socks. Hat—coat. London—England. Paris—France. Scotch—soda (or Scotchtape!).

Names of people also go together. Think of Shirley—and Temple comes to mind. Henry—and Ford, or another person you may think of: Henry—the 8th. Henry—Wadsworth Longfellow. Henry—Jones, a friend of yours. Your reaction will depend upon what combinations you have in your subconscious mind based upon your experiences of the past.

This law illustrates how you remember through natural combinations stored in your subconscious mind.

D. *DESCRIPTIVE QUALITY: PERSON, PLACE OR THING*—Everything in this world can be described.

Quality of a Person—Example: Grandfather is 74 years old, has a long white mustache, loves to listen to good music, does woodworking, takes long walks, loves children. Everything we can recall about this individual is his quality—his appearance and all the facts about him. The more descriptively we think, the more information will come back to mind.

Quality of a Place—If you are telling friends of your visit to Paris, France, here again, the more descriptively you think the more specific details will come back to mind. The Eiffel Tower, the Arc de Triomphe, sidewalk cafes, artists and models. The things you have seen can be mentally reconstructed and vividly explained. Everything you say in regard to Paris denotes its quality.

Quality of an Object—This quality pertains to the description of anything that is inanimate. If you were to describe a Cadillac and a Ford, you would describe them in terms of their differences. The more you use this law of descriptive quality, the more your memory functions, more thoughts come to mind and the more information you have at hand.

4. Retention Through Whole and Part

The Whole and Part relationship is important to remembering ideas. Any given area is the sum total of its parts. The room you are in at this moment is part of the building. The building is part of the location. The location is part of a district. The district is part of the city. The city is part of the county—county, part of the state—state, country—country, continent, etc.

This law has everyday application. As an example, in your home, if you are looking for a misplaced book, don't rush from room to room. You should stop and think: it couldn't be in this room, or this room, or this room. By logical deduction, you would confine the search to one or two areas. In this instance you are starting with the whole area and working down to the individual part.

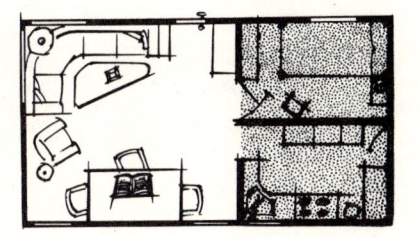

The same thought process is involved using inductive reasoning. You start with a specific item and work up to the general area. You are describing how you build a boat. You start with the keel, ribs, sides, superstructure, each part builds to the total picture.

We use this law constantly when driving from one place to another. We take the most direct path, thus eliminating all the other streets.

As I mentioned, we apply the laws in our everyday lives. You should become aware of these association methods that you naturally apply in acquiring any new knowledge.

Let's remember twelve items by recognizing the logical relationship of each word to the next one. When you read these words, see the logic between each two ideas presented. It is not necessary to think of the laws cited as you read this list. Recognize the logic. These laws are automatically applied.

Read the list three times then write all the words in the exact sequence presented, without referring back to the list. Notice the logical relationships and linking thoughts that go through your mind as you read. Read three times, then cover the list and write the words in the spaces provided.

Ready? Begin!

Matches   _____
Cigarettes   _____
Store   _____
Potatoes   _____
Pot   _____
Pan   _____
Sink   _____
Wrench   _____
Garage   _____
Car   _____
Trip   _____
Voyage   _____

Now, let's analyze this list of words by using our laws of logical association, and see which law or laws apply to each two words.

Matches–Cigarettes . . . *Combinations*. You expect them to go together. Or Cause and Effect could also apply.

Cigarettes—Store . . . *Whole and Part*, because the cigarettes are part of the store's merchandise.

Store—Potatoes . . . *Whole and Part again*, because the potatoes are also part of the store.

Potatoes—Pot . . . *Cause and Effect*. Place potatoes in the pot with water and you produce the effect—cooked potatoes. Also Whole and Part, since the potatoes are now a part of the pot.

Pot—Pan . . . *Synonyms*. We usually think of the pot and pan as the same thing with the same meaning. They are also the same species of cooking utensils.

Pan—Sink . . . *Whole and Part*. When the pan is in the sink, it then becomes a part of the sink.

Sink—Wrench . . . *Cause and Effect*. If something should happen to the pipes under the sink, you would use the wrench to repair it.

Wrench—Garage . . . *Whole and Part*. You think of a garage, and a wrench should be inside that garage.

Garage—Car . . . *Whole and Part*. When the car is in the garage, it is then a part of the garage. Also Combinations, because you think of the two naturally going together.

Car—Trip . . . *Cause and Effect*. You use your car to go on a trip.

Trip—Voyage . . . *Synonyms*. A trip and voyage are terms which mean nearly the same thing to most of us.

In reading over the laws of logical association that apply to the above list of words, you can readily recognize how our minds help us to remember words which are logically connected. This time, try it on your own.

On the following list of words, write the law or laws of logical association which apply to each group of two. Then read the list three times, recognizing how these laws help bring each pair of ideas together in your mind. Then cover the list and test your retention of these twelve words.

Words	Logical Law or Laws that Apply
Restaurant	
Party	
Camera	
Dog	
Fence	

Words	Logical Law or Laws that Apply
Paint	
School	_____
Child	_____
Rain	_____
Umbrella	_____
Beach	_____
Peach	_____

Test Your Retention

On the following lines, list the twelve words which you memorized above.

Words

_____
_____
_____
_____
_____
_____
_____
_____
_____
_____
_____
_____

YOUR SCORE _____

Become familiar with all the laws of logical association. They will make you aware of how ideas come to mind automatically. You will be aided in creating more logical patterns of thinking. Following is a summary of the laws of logical association. Become familiar with them and notice how they will aid your memory.

> # SUMMARY: LAWS OF LOGICAL ASSOCIATION
>
> I. SIMILARITY
>
> > a. *Sight:* Person, place or thing similar to something seen before, such as a car that looks like your own.
> > b. *Sound:* Words that sound similar or rhyme with other words, like ball, hall, call, fall.
> > c. *Synonyms:* Words that have a similar meaning but are not sounded alike, such as big, large, tremendous.
> > d. *Species and Sort:* Form of classification, such as: Animals—dog, cat, horse.
>
> II. CONTRAST: Words or ideas of opposite meaning, like high, low—far, near—large, small.
>
> III. CONTIGUITY
>
> > a. *Cause and Effect:* An action that causes a reaction. Work, money—money, savings—savings, vacation.
> > b. *Chance Happenings:* Happened at a particular time or place by chance. 1492—Columbus discovered America.
> > c. *Combinations:* Things that naturally go together, such as: pen and pencil, bread and butter, salt and pepper.
> > d. *Descriptive Quality:* Describing a person, place or thing. Car—bright red, good mileage, convertible.
>
> IV. WHOLE AND PART: Everything that is part of a whole. Wall, room building, location, city.
>
> *Notice* that all the laws listed under Similarity begin with an "S."
> Three of the laws under Contiguity begin with a "C," the fourth with "D."
> Recognizing this "initial" similarity will assist you in learning all of these Laws.

Apply Laws of Logical Association

The laws of logical association illustrate the way in which your mind classifies and catalogues facts and ideas. When they are applied to memorize new material you then have a point of reasoning to bring this information back to mind when you need it again. You will also find that the application of these Laws will stimulate and bring to mind a tremendous amount of information you would not ordinarily recall. Choose a subject—*the telephone*. On the lines provided below, use your laws of logical association as a check list and write all the information you can remember about *the telephone*, using each law as you come to it.

The Telephone

Similarity of Sight—*Rectangular in shape, with top slanting down; about 5 inches wide by 5 inches high by 8 inches long. Receiver resembles a cradle.*

Sound _____
_____
_____

Synonyms _____
_____
_____

Species and Sort _____
_____
_____

Contrast _____
_____
_____

Contiguity, Cause and Effect _____
_____
_____

Chance Happenings _____
_____
_____

Combinations _____
_____
_____

Descriptive Quality _____
_____
_____

Whole and Part _____
_____
_____
_____

MEMORY SYSTEMS

Chapter **Three**

Can you imagine what would happen in the Pentagon if it were necessary to rummage through unsorted stacks and stacks of paper to find certain letters or printed forms? Fortunately, there is a very efficient filing system. But suppose there were none. The result would be chaos!

Your brain is just as busy and complex a place as the Pentagon. But it must do more things simultaneously! You are fortunate that you don't have to go to a separate file room to find information; you possess nature's most perfect filing cabinet—your memory. But it's up to you to become a good file clerk!

There is no other faculty more desirable than a dependable memory. No matter how much information and knowledge you may possess, it is useless if you cannot remember it when you need it. Without a system for remembering, your brain is just as chaotic as would be the Pentagon without its filing system. In contrast, the individual who has trained his memory puts each fact into its place, labels it, and knows where to look for it when it is needed again.

By training your memory, you will learn how to do just this: *classify and file material in your mind, so that when you need the information, it is where it should be—at your fingertips!*

The best way to make your memory into an efficient filing cabinet is to develop systems. Just as there are cross files and indexes, so there are a number of different systems to help your memory. Sometimes you will use one, sometimes another. Occasionally they will overlap.

The memory systems you are learning in this course will help you to have a good memory. Use them often!

Your mind contains many automatic systems to aid your memory. You have used these systems since you were only a few days old. You started remembering through patterns of sight, sound, touch, taste and smell. As you grew older, these senses became more developed. You recognized faces, voices, foods and objects.

When you started the first grade, you learned a system which eventually led to a means of communication—the alphabet. These 26 letters have sounds. Combining these letters, you learned to recognize and remember words, and the words became meaningful. Without your alphabet, there would be no combinations to recognize—no words, no communication through these printed symbols.

In this chapter, we will discuss Five Basic Memory Systems which you will use throughout your memory training course. In all these systems you will notice that it is important that you use your imagination constantly.

Let us first define imagination. What is it?

The imagination is the process in your mind that produces an object or idea in your mind's eye. The object is not really there, you just imagine it is. If I put a book in front of you and you can see it, this is not the imagination. But if I said, picture the book on the ceiling, do you see it? If you do, then you are using your imagination. This technique of imagination, or visualization, of objects or ideas which are not actually in view will be used to a very high degree in this course. As was discussed previously, most individuals are eye-minded and therefore can memorize more readily by visualization.

MEMORY SYSTEMS 31

Before going on to our Five Systems, let us take an exercise to develop your imagination. If I asked you how long it would take you to memorize 20 objects in a perfect sequence and to know them backward and forward, you may say 10 minutes, 10 hours, 10 days . . . never! I'll show you that by knowing how to associate ideas through a definite memory system, you can memorize 20 items in two minutes' time.

Now, without repetition, we will start to learn a system by tying just 10 items together. Use your imagination, logic and your ability to observe the placement of the items.

Here is an illustration of 10 objects. See how quickly you can tie these pictures together in your mind. First see the **glass** on top of the **car**. Then see the car hit the **ball**. The ball bounces up the **ladder**. Sitting on top of the ladder is a **bird**, the bird flies off onto the top of a **door**, the door falls over on an **elephant**. The elephant wraps his trunk around a **tree**, the tree lands on the back of the **ship** and the ship hits a **table**. Go through the entire picture, associating each two items together as you come to them. **When you have finished, turn the page and take a test of your retention. Visualize as you recall!**

Test Your Memory

List all 10 objects below which you associated together on the preceding page, in the exact order in which you memorized them. Record your score.

_____   _____   _____   _____
_____   _____   _____   _____
_____   _____

                                                      Your Score _____

You have applied the technique correctly if all the items came back to mind quickly. If one or two items did not come to mind, then go over the entire list again, strengthening each association by applying more action between each two objects. Exaggerate. Make large mental pictures, even ridiculous ones! They needn't be logical so long as the associations help you to remember.

Test yourself within the next 24 hours. All 10 items should still be tied securely in your mind. You will find that as you practice this technique, you will get better and faster mental pictures.

For more permanent retention of facts to be remembered, you should review any new material within 24 hours and not later than 48 hours. As you review, see the relationships once again, with as much action as originally applied. You can even add more active associations.

A week later or even months later, this information will come to mind. Some material, for more permanent retention, may have to be reviewed periodically. This will depend on the strength of your association or how abstract the material may be.

Five Systems

I. Cue Systems

The method you have just applied to some simplified items will be the basis of a system which I call a *Cue System*. That is, tying a series of cues together to bring back information when needed.

Our definition of a cue is anything that is in an abbreviated form and which serves as a springboard to bring information back to mind. The cue correctly chosen represents the information. When this cue is recalled it should bring to mind all the supporting facts.

MEMORY SYSTEMS

We use cues in our everyday lives. If your phone rings, what is the cue? Yes—answer it. You are driving down the street: the light turns red—cue to stop. Someone mentions your name: cue—you respond.

The actor on stage listens for cue words given by another performer, then reacts. Actors have both word cues and physical cues. A word cue could be "Aunt Margaret," or a physical cue could be the slam of a door — then they react.

In public speaking, the professional would not refer to a lengthy outline while speaking. Instead, he or she would merely memorize 6 to 30 meaningful cues representing all of the information. This condensed series of cues replaces a cumbersome outline. The number of cues will be determined by the length of the speech and the speaker's knowledge of the subject.

The speaker has another advantage in using cues. The speaker could review a complete talk within a few moments just by reviewing a list of cue words written on a 3 x 5 card. If they have given many talks, they might keep a file in which each specific talk is represented on a 3 x 5 card.

A person who remembers anecdotes or quotations uses this same cue system. Perhaps you have experienced this: you are trying to think of an anecdote and it just won't come to mind. Another person starts to tell his anecdote, and right in the middle of his story he says one word which reminds you of the anecdote you tried so hard to think of moments before. This word is the cue.

The student taking an essay exam must remember cues. These cues bring back the total concept. Without cues he may leave out important segments.

Cues are used even more in an objective type exam. Important cues are hidden within the questions. In a multiple choice question, for example, the student must be able to recognize the right cue among many misleading cues in order to choose the correct answer.

To represent logical progression of ideas, cues will be associated in sequence. You will notice that these ideas will automatically go together in your mind because of the logic between each two ideas.

Memorize this list of cues in order by noticing the relationship of each idea to the next one on the list.

Boats
Auto
Mountain
Gun

Store
Baby
Train
Desert
Telephone
Suitcase

Close the book and see how many of these cues you can remember. The cues must be in their exact sequence. Now see how close you came by checking your mental list with the one above.

These 10 cues were extracted from the following story. Read this story and see how the cues stand out as the main ideas represented.

MY VACATION

At the first vantage point we came upon a harbor filled with **boats,** each blending majestically with the sea. There were outboards, cabin cruisers and sail boats. Far off in the distance we could see a freighter slowly ploughing its way eastward.

Turning away, each of us silently wished we could be sailing the seas. But for landlubbers the **auto** was the handiest form of transportation. Ours was a blue station wagon and it had given us hundreds of carefree, enjoyable miles on this trip.

Leaving the inlet and wending our way up the **mountain,** the higher altitude, too, had its form of majesty. Tall graceful trees and thick underbrush carpeted the entire landscape. Mountains are nature at its colorful best.

Suddenly someone shouted, "Let's do some plinking." We pulled over into a small clearing. Frank got the **gun** from the rear trunk as we set up a few targets of wood chips. The crack of the small gun echoed throughout the small canyon.

About 20 miles further up the road we came to a quaint village **store.** The building looked as though it had been standing since the last silver strike many years before. We could see a multitude of merchandise through the windows as we curiously approached the entrance. The store was tended by a lone woman.

In the corner was a **baby** busily playing in a large packing case. The baby was about 18 months old and had dark brown hair and large brown eyes. Her contentment was remarkable. It was difficult to part company with her.

At the summit, we could see the broad sweep of a valley. In the middle of it a long freight **train** was slowly inching its way. We counted over 60 freight cars. It was surprising that a train could look so small and unimpressive. Perhaps we would meet it again.

MEMORY SYSTEMS 35

>The descent would eventually lead us to the entrance of the Mojave Desert. The **desert** is unique and must be treated with much respect. We could feel the temperature slowly rising and the long straight desert roads of the desert floor were coming into view.
>
>At the next gas stop we decided to **telephone** ahead for reservations. The telephone was the old fashioned type and the connection seemed to take forever. A person could really be in for trouble without a telephone here.
>
>Arriving at our destination three hours later, we unloaded the car. **Suitcases** in hand we triumphantly marched into the hotel lobby.

Although these cues represented a story about an individual's vacation, it could just as well have been a chapter of history text, a sales presentation, an interesting article or book which you had read. You will see that cues are used throughout our memory training course for the retention of all types of material.

II. *Visual Key System*

Our *Visual Key System* refers to visualizing an object or idea and keying other information to it. The memory is aided by thinking of the original object or idea, and immediately the item or idea that was associated with it will come to mind.

We compare our Visual Key System to a file cabinet that has many drawers. If an item is placed in a particular drawer, when you need it again you know exactly what drawer to look in.

At this part of our memory course you will learn a series of Visual Keys. These Visual Keys will be given numerical values. Our Visual Key System is a method of associating words with numbers, so that when you need information you can recall it either in or out of numerical sequence.

As an example of how we can bring numbers and objects together, we are going to visualize the following 10 words going together with numbers from 1 to 10. Concentrate on each one individually to get a clear picture of the number and the object going together. Use your imagination combined with action wherever possible or logic wherever possible.

We begin by visualizing the number *1* swinging on a HUT. Once you have established a strong mental image of the number *1* swinging on the HUT, at a later time when you think of number *1* the HUT will reappear with it. It works both ways, because when you think of the HUT, then the number *1* will be in your picture on the HUT. Now associate all 10 words in the same manner.

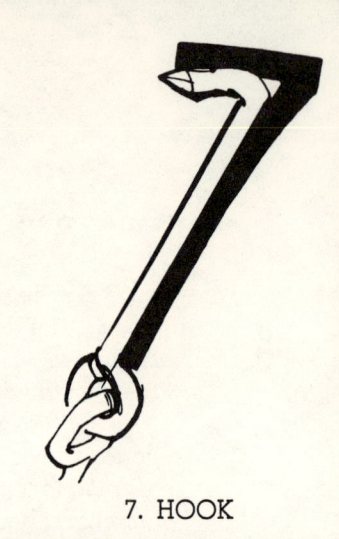

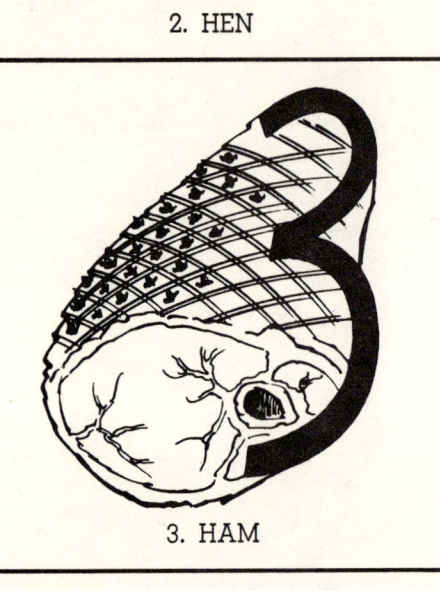

1. HUT
2. HEN
3. HAM
4. HARE
5. HILL
6. JAY
7. HOOK
8. HIVE
9. APE
10. TOES

Visual Key Words 1–10

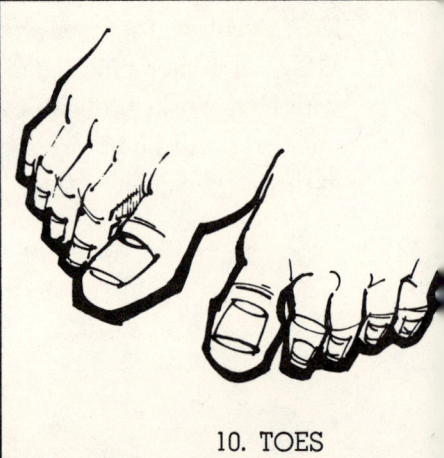

MEMORY SYSTEMS 37

Now, test your retention of these 10 words. What was number one? Number two? Number three? Number seven? Number nine? Number six? Number four? Number ten? Number five? Number eight? Now, look away and recall in a perfect sequence all 10 items, from number one through number ten.

As you read or think of the number, you should see a clear mental picture of the object which you associated with the number. You should feel the stimulus of the association coming back to mind. In the next chapter, we will expand upon this Visual Key System and learn a fascinating, easily acquired method which will enable us to memorize 100 facts, 1,000 facts, or more if needed, in or out of numerical sequence, and with a minimum of effort.

III. Initial System of Remembering

The *Initial System of Remembering* is a very easy system to understand and apply because all of us have been using it since childhood. About the age of five, we recognized that P.D. represented Police Department; F.D.—Fire Department; P.O.—Post Office; U.S.A.—United States of America; F.B.I.—Federal Bureau of Investigation. As you grew older, you may have read about one of our Presidents, F.D.R. These initials, of course, referred to Franklin Delano Roosevelt. Other memorable initials include: R.P.M.—revolutions per minute; C.O.—Commanding Officer; A.T.&T.—American Telephone and Telegraph Company, and G.M.—General Motors.

Initials are used in most any area of learning that can be mentioned. It is a system of abbreviated symbols universally applied. However, very few people use their own creative ingenuity to aid their memory by applying this system of extracting initials from different types of facts to be remembered.

The Initial System of cues refers to the technique of extracting the first letter of each word in a list of facts to remembered, and making a *word* from these letters. This *word* or combination of letters holds the entire list of facts in your mind.

The combination of letters does not necessarily have to spell a recognizable word. Many times, just remembering two letters or a combination of letters that means nothing to the average person is all that is necessary. However, when you think of the *word* or combination of letters, each letter must bring to mind the desired information.

As an example, we can use the Initial System to remember the names

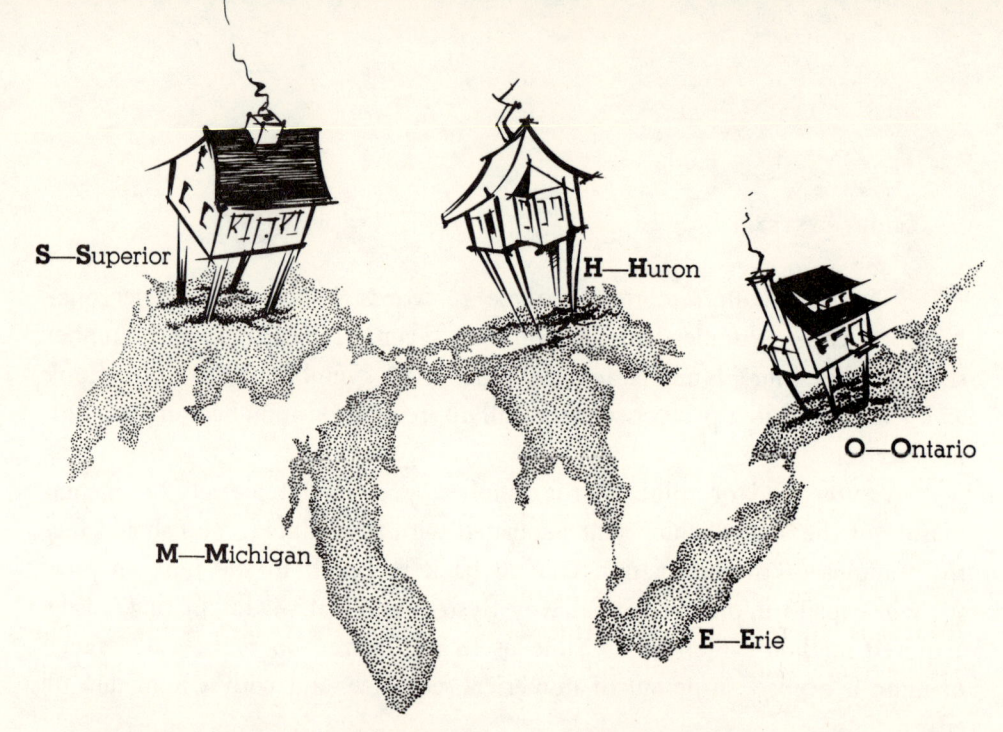

S—Superior
H—Huron
O—Ontario
M—Michigan
E—Erie

Ⓟ–**P**ostmaster General

A–**A**ttorney General

T–**T**reasury, Secretary

T–**T**ransportation Secretary

S–**S**tate, Secretary

A–**A**griculture, Secretary

C–**C**ommerce, Secretary

H–**H**ealth, and Human Services, Secretary

H–**H**ousing, Secretary

I – **I**nterior, Secretary

L–**L**abor, Secretary

D–**D**efense, Secretary

E–**E**nergy, Assistant to the President

of the five Great Lakes. Think of the word HOMES, and each letter represents one of our Great Lakes.

Just picture, mentally, five huge HOMES surrounding the Great Lakes, and when you wish to remember them, the word HOMES will come back to mind. Each letter will recall one of the five Great Lakes.

Another example, and a very practical one, is the use of the Initial System to permanently remember the names of the 11 Cabinet posts in the President's Cabinet.

Just associate three simple words—PATTS A CHHILD**E** and here is what the letters in these three words represent.

Notice that in the illustration, we have pictured the President as he PATTS A CHHILD**E**. When you think of these three words again, you can name all 12 posts in the President's Cabinet. (The circle around the letter P indicates that the Post Master General is no longer a Cabinet post.) you will retain this information for the rest of your life.

The Initial System of remembering is applied to all types of material. In the study of medicine and law, there is unlimited application of this technique. Use it whenever possible. It's quick and it's effective! Remember, review and reinforce your associations within 24 hours.

IV. *Cues Using Logic and Imagination*

A method of mixing logical cues and imagination will play a dominant role in your memory training program. As an example, let us learn the names of the nine planets in the order of their distance from the sun. They are: *Mercury, Venus, Earth, Mars, Jupiter, Saturn, Uranus, Neptune, Pluto.*

Some of these names already represent something concrete in your own mind. Others may be somewhat abstract, and for these you will use your

MEMORY SYSTEMS 39

imagination and make it meaningful by choosing a picture word which is close *in sound* to the name of the planet.

Mercury is the first planet, closest to the sun. Let us establish a good picture for the planet Mercury. You may say that Mercury means a car . . . the god of speed . . . the mercury in a thermometer. In this instance, we will use the god of speed to represent Mercury.

See *Mercury* (the god of speed) racing away from the sun. The next planet is *Venus*, so see Mercury chasing Venus. The next planet is *Earth*. Can't you see Venus racing around the Earth? The earth is inhabited by Martians, to represent the planet *Mars*. The Martians are drinking mint Juleps (for *Jupiter*) which spill onto a piece of Satin (for *Saturn*). The satin is being cleansed by Rain (for *Uranus*), which moves over to fall on *Neptune*, the king of the sea, filling his crown with water. Neptune takes his scepter and pokes the little puppy dog, *Pluto*.

Notice the illustration which gives a complete picture of the planets in a perfect sequence. Then close the book and test your retention of the planets.

Any list of facts such as the planets can be associated successfully in this manner. Test your retention of the planets tomorrow and you will find that if the associations were made correctly, then all the planets will come back to mind. A further review in the future will keep the information permanently fixed in mind.

V. Observation and Association

Observation is the faculty with which we receive a conscious impression through our eyes. Association is actively bringing two facts or ideas together for the purpose of recalling them together.

You practiced this technique of observation and association when you memorized 10 objects at the beginning of this chapter to develop your imagination. Use the same technique to memorize the following series of objects in a perfect sequence. Numbers are not important in this exercise.

Associate the objects together beginning with the first two and continuing on across the top line. See the broom hit the shoe, the shoe kicks the book, the book opens and out comes a feather. Continue on your own. When you reach the end of the first line, associate the object on the end with the first object on the second line. When you reach the end of the second line, associate the object on the end with the first object on the third line, and so forth. They should be memorized in a perfect sequence from left to right on each line.

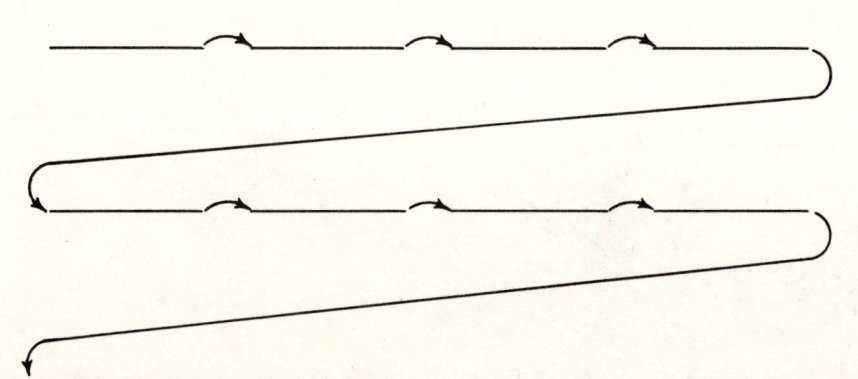

When you have finished the exercise, turn the page and test your retention. Try for 100%! Ready? Begin!

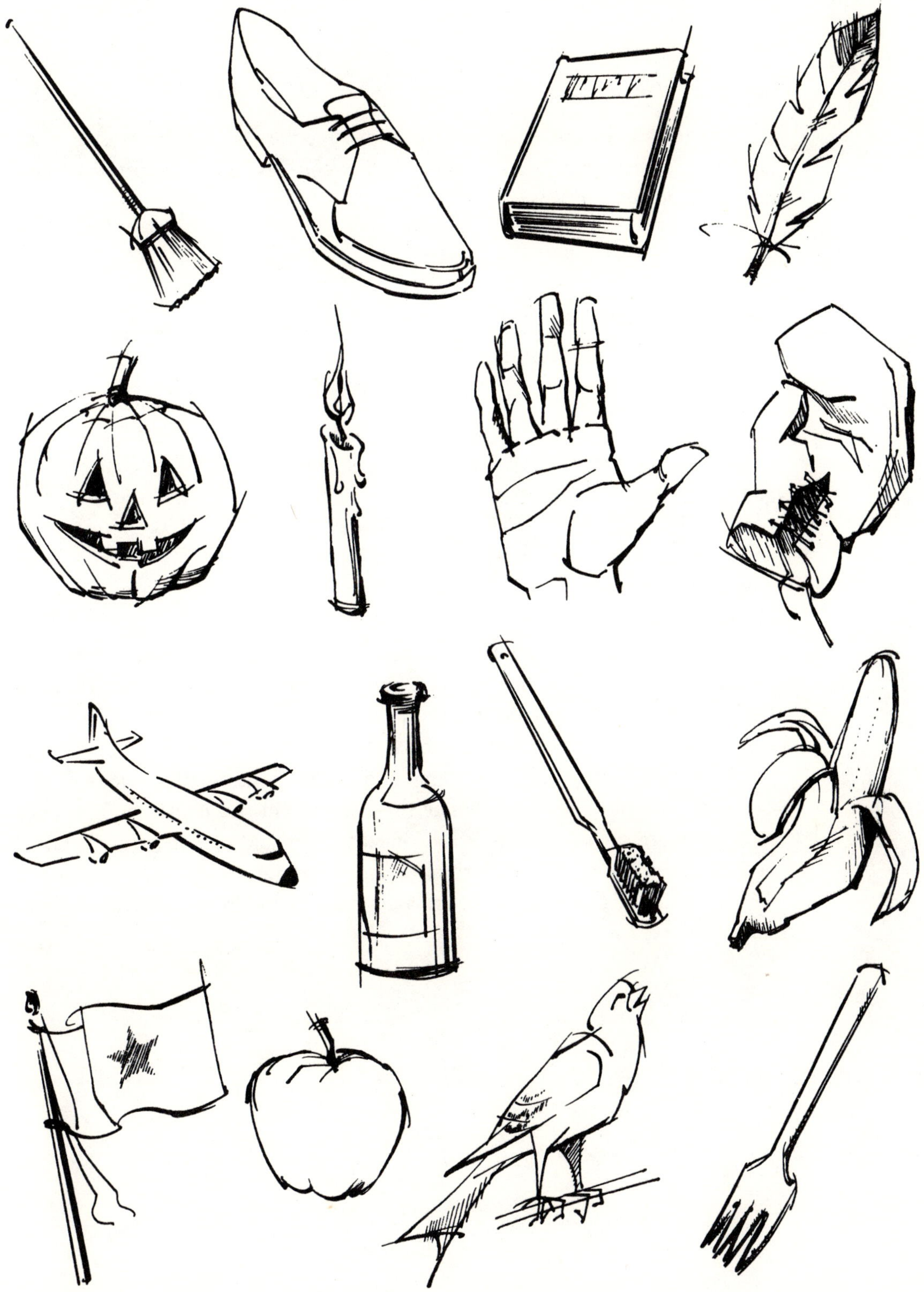

Test Your Memory

Write the objects which you have just memorized in their proper positions on the following lines. Then compare your list with the original illustration. Record your score.

_____	_____	_____	_____
_____	_____	_____	_____
_____	_____	_____	_____
_____	_____	_____	_____

Your Score _____

After you have actively associated these 16 items, go over them once again to notice their position and details such as which way was the shoe pointing, left or right? Was the candle lit? Which hand was illustrated, right or left? How many teeth in the jack-o-lantern's head? When you write these items, revisualize them as clearly as you can, noticing once again the position and details.

Throughout this memory training course, you will be given exercises to practice which utilize one, two or more of the basic systems which were illustrated in this chapter. In many instances they will be used in combination to retain different types of material.

Visualizing, listening, reasoning and creating associations all call for good concentration. As you practice the exercises in this course you will develop your ability to concentrate. Concentration and retention go hand in hand, because you must concentrate to remember anything.

REMEMBER! Concentration prevents mind-wandering and increases retentive ability.

LET'S LEARN
A SYSTEM

Chapter **Four**

Throughout your entire educational life you have witnessed a procession of systems to fulfill your academic needs.

It all began when you were six years of age and in the first grade. You were learning systems which at that time seemed complex. One system that you learned was a series of symbols: A, B, C, D, E, F, G, H, I, J, K, L, M, N, O, P, Q, R, S, T, U, V, W, X, Y, Z. Later you learned that these symbols are letters of the English alphabet. These letters have sounds and the sounds are combined to form words. Without this system, you could not read.

Then your teacher presented numerical digits: *1, 2, 3, 4, 5, 6, 7, 8, 9, 0*. She showed you how to count and as the days went by she showed you that you put *1* and *2* together and it creates the number *12* . . . a *3* and *4* together and it creates the number *34*.

As you continued to learn you were instructed that you can add *17* and *17* to equal *34*. You progressed on to *7 x 7* equals *49*, which gave you a system of multiplication. Then it was pointed out that *2* divided into *10* goes *5* times. This was called the system of division.

All of this basic knowledge is designed to help you think and apply logical patterns of learning to your everyday life.

Now that you realize that you have learned systems in the past, you are going to expand this basic knowledge of systems of numbers and letters into a memory system which will help you retain numerical data, facts and ideas. At the same time, this system will help develop your concentration and your ability to imagine, classify and associate ideas.

Our system, called a *Numerical Alphabet*, is an organized method primarily designed to retain numerical data. Now, let us learn the method.

Here we have numbers from 1 to 0:

1 2 3 4 5 6 7 8 9 0

Notice that most people have no difficulty remembering numbers when there is a logical progression such as *1234, 2468, 1357*, or when the combinations are meaningful such as *1492* (Columbus), *1776* (Declaration of Independence). These well-known combinations can be associated and recalled easily.

When the combinations are abstract such as *150829*, this means nothing to the average individual and is therefore difficult to retain. We're going to make numbers meaningful and visual through the use of our Numerical Alphabet.

Carefully notice that we are associating numbers and the letters of our English alphabet together. The letters of the alphabet are related to numbers in the following way. (*Make a special point of understanding the reasons below*):

NUMBER	LETTER	REASON
1	t	The basic downstroke in a *1* and the *t* are similar.

LET'S LEARN A SYSTEM 45

NUMBER	LETTER	REASON
2	n	The two strokes in *n* make it a natural choice for *2*.
3	m	With three strokes, *m* has been chosen to represent *3* for the same reason.
4	R	The strongest sound in the word four is *R*. Also, the fourth letter in the word fou*r* is *R*.
5	L	*L* is the roman numeral for *50*. Drop the *o* and *L* represents *5*. Also, Lincoln is on a $5.00 bill. *L* for *5*.
6	J	Reverse a *J* and it resembles a *6*.
7	K	The first stroke of a written *K* resembles a *7*. *K like on a*
8	f	A small written *f* has two loops, resembling an *8*. *Kellog's Cereal Box*
9	P	A reversed *P* resembles a *9*.
0	z	The first letter of the word zero is *z*. Also, *z* is the last letter of our alphabet and *o* is the last numerical digit.

The Basic Numerical Alphabet looks like this:

1	2	3	4	5	6	7	8	9	0
t	n	m	R	L	J	K	f	P	z

Look at the above letters and notice that all the letters below the numbers are consonants. In contrast to our consonants we have vowels. The vowels that most people are familiar with are a, e, i, o, u. For our purpose we're going to add W, H, Y, which is easy to remember just by asking yourself, WHY?

These vowels will have *no numerical value*. All the consonants in the English alphabet will have numerical significance, but all these vowels will have no numerical value.

Before going any further, let's find out what a Numerical Alphabet does. We can take words and translate words into numbers. As an example, the word MAT equals 31: the M for 3, A is a vowel, and therefore has no number value, and the T has the value of 1.

MAT
3 — 1

The word JET becomes 61, because the J is 6, the E is a vowel with no number value, and T is 1.

JET
6 — 1

The word POT is 91, the P is 9, the O a vowel, and the T is 1.

POT
9 — 1

When words have more consonants you will notice that the number is longer. Take the word PAPER. The P is 9, the A is a vowel with no number, the P again is 9, the E another vowel (so no number), and the R is 4.

PAPER
9 — 9 — 4

Let's take a word with more consonants, such as PRINT: P for 9, R for 4, N for 2, T for 1.

PRINT
9 4 — 2 1

Isn't that simple? Now let's add the other consonants of the alphabet which have not been mentioned. They also will have numerical value. The way we are going to accomplish this is by recognizing that the various letters of the alphabet have sounds and some letters have sounds which are similar, such as: the T which sounds like a D. Prove this to yourself. Say the letters T and D, noticing that your tongue touches the upper palate in the same position when you say both letters.

The following chart will illustrate the consonants which sound similar. Notice that the similar sounding consonants have the same number value.

	LETTERS OF SIMILAR SOUND	EXAMPLES
1 = t	Since the letters *t* and *d* sound similar, the *d* will also have the numerical value of *1*.	*t*en *d*en
2 = n	No other letters with similar sound. Therefore, *n* is the only letter to represent number *2*.	
3 = m	No other letters with similar sound. Therefore, *m* is the only letter to represent number *3*.	
4 = R	No other letters with similar sound. Therefore, *R* is the only letter to represent number *4*.	
5 = L	No other letters with similar sound. Therefore, *L* is the only letter to represent number *5*.	
6 = J	The letter *J* and a soft *G* sound alike. A soft *G* as in words like *G*eorge, *G*ene, *g*em, will also be given the number value of *6*.	*J*ean *G*ene (sound–*J*ene)
7 = K	The letter *K* and the hard *C* sound alike. Therefore, the hard *C* as in words like *c*ar, *c*oat, *c*ane, will also represent the number *7*.	*K*itten *C*at (sound–*K*at)
8 = f	The letters *f* and *v* are similar in sound. Notice words such as knife when made plural becomes knives. The *f* changes to a *v* as life–lives. The *ph* combination of letters sounds exactly like the *f*, in words such as *ph*oto, *ph*rase, *ph*ilosophy. Therefore since *ph* sounds like *f*, it will also represent the number *8*.	wi*f*e wi*v*es *ph*one (sounds like *f*one)
9 = P	*P* and *B* have similar sounds. Notice when you pronounce the letters *P* and *B* your lips are in the same position. Therefore, both letters *P* and *B* will represent the number *9*. An easy way to remember that the *B* will also represent the number *9* is to notice that a *P* looks like a small *b* upside down.	*p*et *b*et
0 = Z	*Z* and *S* sound very similar in words such as ro*s*e, no*s*e, clo*s*e. The soft *C* also has the sound of *S* and will have the number value of zero. Notice words like *c*ent, *c*ereal, *c*inder–the *C* sounds like the letter *S*, therefore it is called a soft *C*.	ha*z*e toe*s* (sounds like to*z*e) *s*it *c*ity (sounds like *s*ity)

Now, let's take a look at the Numerical Alphabet with its additions.

\multicolumn{10}{c	}{NUMERICAL ALPHABET}
1	2	3	4	5	6	7	8	9	0
t d	n	m	R	L	J G*	K C**	f v ph	P B	z s c*

* Soft Sound
** Hard Sound
Note: Vowels have no number value: a, e, i, o, u, plus w, h, y.

To aid in learning the Numerical Alphabet we are going to practice translating words into numbers according to their sounds. It is important to remember that this system is based *completely* on the phonetic (sound) relationship of the letters of our alphabet. Therefore, we are going to translate all words back into numbers according to the sounds of the letters. If a "gh" in a word such as "rough" sounds like an "F," you translate it as an "F," which is the number 8.

If the letter "C" in the word "cent" sounds like the letter "S," it will be translated into an "S," equalling the number 0.

Translate the following words back into numbers according to their sounds. You may refer to the Numerical Alphabet if needed. Remember that the vowels A, E, I, O, U and W, H, Y are not translated into numbers.

Examples: FAN   RAIN   PAINT
            8 2 4 2 9   9 2 1

Now you're on your own. Practice on the following list of words. At the end of the exercise you will find these words again, with their correct numbers. Do not refer to the answers until you have completed translating these words into numbers.

EXERCISE 1

MOP _____	RAKE _____	LAKE _____
CAPE _____	POLE _____	LAWN _____
OIL _____	CIRCUS _____	WORLD _____
HAND _____	FILM _____	MONEY _____

LET'S LEARN A SYSTEM

49

Now compare your answers with the correct ones given below. Then write your score in the space provided.

ANSWERS TO EXERCISE I

MOP	39	RAKE	47	LAKE	57
CAPE	79	POLE	95	LAWN	52
OIL	5	CIRCUS	0470	WORLD	451
HAND	21	FILM	853	MONEY	32

Be careful when translating these next 12 words. *Translate the consonants the way they are sounded.* Notice hard and soft sounds. Do not look at the answers until you have completed Exercise II.

EXERCISE II

BALL	____	LABEL	____	CAPTAIN	____
POTATO	____	CAMERA	____	FAUCET	____
CABIN	____	LEVER	____	PASTE	____
FACTORY	____	TIDE	____	GENTLEMEN	____

Compare your answers with the ones which follow.

ANSWERS TO EXERCISE II

BALL	95	LABEL	595	CAPTAIN	7912
POTATO	911	CAMERA	734	FAUCET	801
CABIN	792	LEVER	584	PASTE	901
FACTORY	8714	TIDE	11	GENTLEMEN	621532

YOUR SCORE ____

Did you answer 955 for Ball instead of 95? Remember that you were instructed to translate the words into numbers by the sound of the word. When you say Ball, you only hear one L, because the two together blend together. You don't say *Bal-l* . . . you say what sounds like *bal*. (If you are in doubt as to the pronunciation of a particular word, check the word in a self-pronouncing dictionary.)

In Chapter Three, you used your imagination to tie a number to a particular object. Remember? Number "1" was swinging on a HUT, number "2" was our HEN, and number "3" was a HAM. Now translate that same list of ten words back into numbers according to your Numerical Alphabet. Here is the list again:

1. HUT _____   6. JAY _____
2. HEN _____   7. HOOK _____
3. HAM _____   8. HIVE _____
4. HARE _____   9. APE _____
5. HILL _____   10. TOES _____

Notice something interesting taking place? Right! These words came out in exact numerical sequence from one to ten. If you translated the word Hill to number 55, say the word aloud and you will hear one *L* pronounced —*HIL*. Therefore, the double consonant *LL* in HI*LL* can only be translated into one *L*—number 5.

You are now at the beginning of a system which we call the *Bornstein Visual Keys*. You will notice that these Keys are directly related to the number because in the numerical Alphabet the consonants represent these certain numbers. This system will be discussed in more detail later on in this chapter. Before we continue with the Bornstein Visual Key System, we are going to complete the Numerical Alphabet.

At this point, there are several consonants that have not been given numerical values. There are also letter combinations that are pronounced similar to the letters in our basic Numerical Alphabet. The following letters will be given numerical values because of their similar sounds to our basic Numerical Alphabet.

The combination "th" will also have the value of number *1*. Notice that this "th" in words such as *th*ose, *th*ere, *th*em, *th*ese, is softer than the "t" in words such as *t*oy, *t*oo, *T*om. Whether a word has "t" or the "th" together, it will still have the value of number *1*.

The N, M, R, and L remain alone.

The number *6* with its letters "J" and "G" have several combinations also to represent the number *6*. Consider "dg" as in e*dg*e, ri*dg*e, le*dg*e. Notice that the "d" and "g" blend together and sound like the "J": e*dg*e—*eje*,

LET'S LEARN A SYSTEM

ri*dge*—ri*je*, le*dge*—le*je*. The "sh," "ch" and "tch" combinations will also be represented by the number *6*, because of their similarity to the sound of "J."

The number 7 also has several letters that sound similar to the letter "K." Hard "G" as in *g*o, *g*et, *g*ood. The letter "Q" as in *q*uiet, *q*uick, *Q*ueen has a "ku" or "kw" sound. The "ng" combination found at the end of words, as in ri*ng*, ki*ng*, si*ng*, blend together, with the emphasis placed on the "G." Therefore, "ng" combinations will have the numerical value of the number 7.

Notice that the soft sounds come from the forward part of the mouth. *S* as in *s*weet, *j* as in *j*am, soft *c* as in *c*ity, *sh* as in *sh*oe, *ch* as in *ch*ampion, *tch* as in di*tch*, soft *g* as in *g*entle.

The hard sounds (gutteral sounds) come from the back of the throat. Hard *g* as in *g*o, *g*et, *g*ot. *K* as in *k*ite, hard *c* as in *c*ar, *q* as in *q*uick. Notice that you have to open your mouth to get these sounds out.

The letter "X" will not be included in the Numerical Alphabet at this time because it has two basic consonant sounds—a *K* and *S*. For example, the word WAX sounds like WAKS. Translated into a number, WAX becomes 70: k, s. The word TAX sounds like TAKS. *TAX* becomes 170 . . . *FIX* would become 870.

At this time, we will only use consonants that represent one number. However, in later application of our Numerical System the letter X may be used.

Learn the following chart and know it well. This Numerical Alphabet will aid greatly in learning our system called "Visual Keys." The Numerical Alphabet and its application to remembering numbers will be discussed in a later chapter.

COMPLETE NUMERICAL ALPHABET									
1	2	3	4	5	6	7	8	9	0
t d th	n	m	R	L	J G* dg sh ch tch	K C** G** Q ng	f v ph	P B	z s c*

* Soft Sounds
** Hard Sounds
Note: Vowels have no number value: a, e, i, o, u, plus w, h, y.

Numbers *6* and *7* have more combinations to remember than the other numbers. Here is an aid to learning *6* and *7*.

To remember the values of number *6* memorize this sentence: 6—*J*oan and *G*eorge Ju*dg*ed a *Sh*y *Ch*ild's ma*tch*.

To remember the values of number *7* memorize this sentence: 7—*K*ittens and *C*ats *G*o *Q*uarreli*ng*.

Run these two sentences through your mind several times, picturing each sentence as you read. These two sentences will act as a check list for remembering the consonants that represent number *6* and number *7*.

Translate the following list of 10 words back into numbers according to the way they sound.

TIDE_____	TISSUE
	(sound: TISHU) _____
TIN _____	TAG _____
TAM _____	TAFFY
	(sound: TAFY) _____
TIRE _____	TUB _____
TAIL _____	NOSE _____

If your translations are correct, you should have recorded numbers progressing from *11* to *20*. These last 10 words together with the words HUT, HEN, HAM, HARE, HILL, JAY, HOOK, HIVE, APE and TOES, which you previously translated into numbers from *1* to *10*, are the first 20 words in our system called "Visual Keys."

Before we go on to apply this system, let's once again define a *Visual Key*. A *Visual Key* is a definite item to which another item may be securely associated. We call this Visual because you should be able to visualize the first item clearly in mind. The word Key is used because the first item can be *keyed* to another item through the process of association within your own mind.

When applying the Visual Key System, you will notice that the Key Words remain constant, while the information which you wish to retain will change from subject to subject. We can compare this system to a filing system whereby we will have file drawers in which to keep facts and ideas. This information, when needed, can be recalled at will by simply thinking of the file drawer which we call a Visual Key.

LET'S LEARN A SYSTEM

Here are the suggested illustrations of how you should visualize your first 20 Key Words. Know them well. In your spare time, call these words in a perfect sequence, from *1* to *20*: HUT, HEN, HAM, HARE, HILL, etc., then call them out of sequence—number *10* is TOES, *15* is TAIL, *6* is JAY, *9* is APE, and so forth.

Practice until you can call all *20* words back to memory without hesitation. Remember that the numerical factor of these Key Words is based upon our Numerical Alphabet. If you are in doubt as to number *18*, think of a "T" and "F"; place a vowel in between: TAF, and the basic sound will remind you of TAFFY. "T" and "M"; place the vowel in between and the TAM comes to mind for number *13*. Practice in your spare moments by calling your Visual Keys to mind from HUT through NOSE.

Visual Key Words 1–20

1. HUT

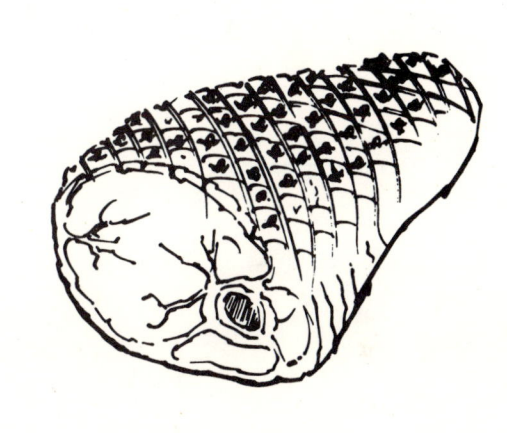

3. HAM

2. HEN

4. HARE

5. HILL

6. JAY

7. HOOK

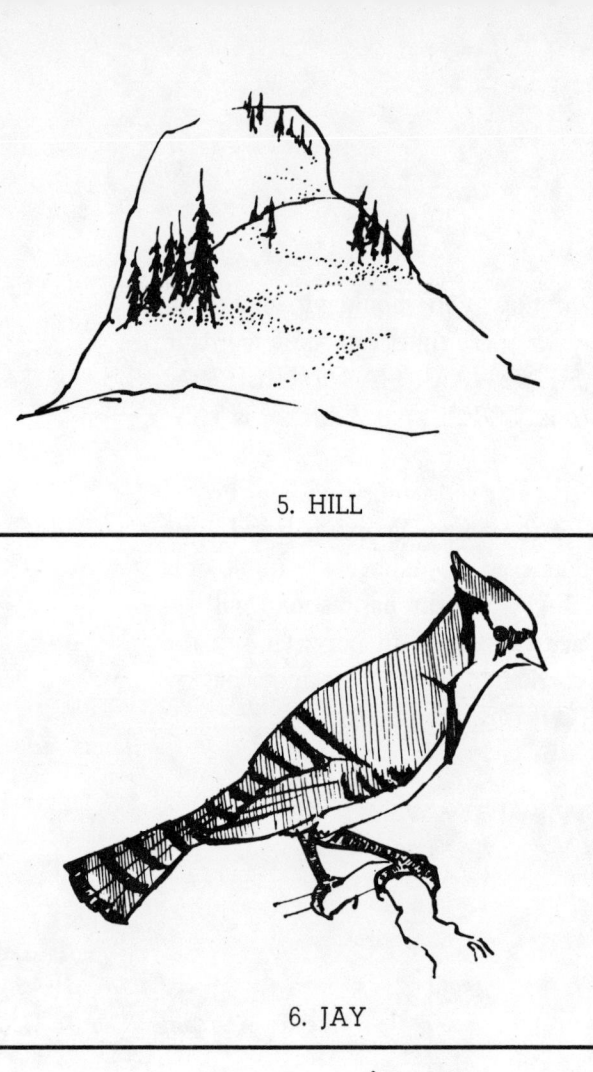

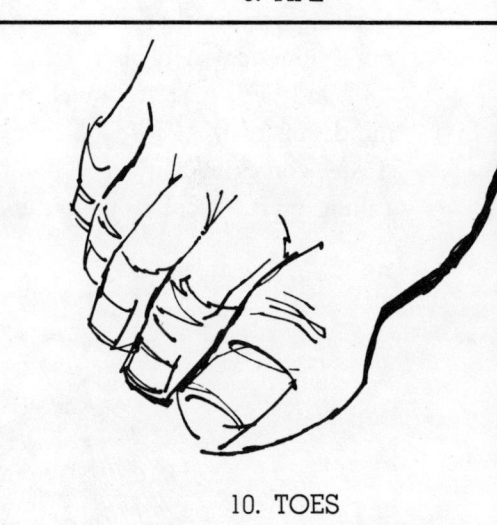

8. HIVE

9. APE

10. TOES

11. TIDE

12. TIN

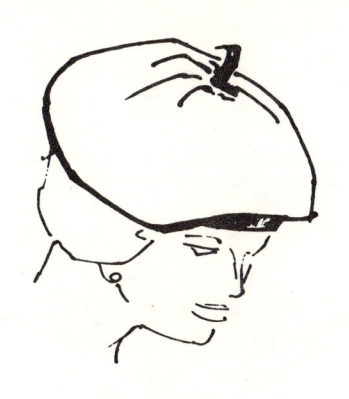

13. TAM

17. TAG

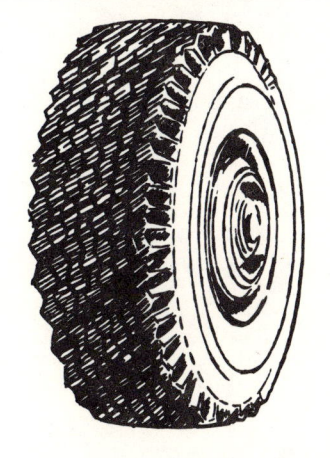

14. TIRE

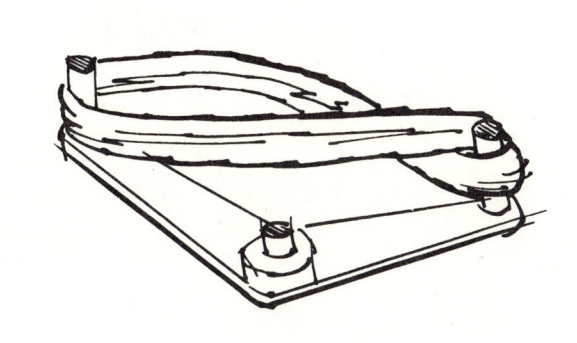

18. TAFFY

15. TAIL

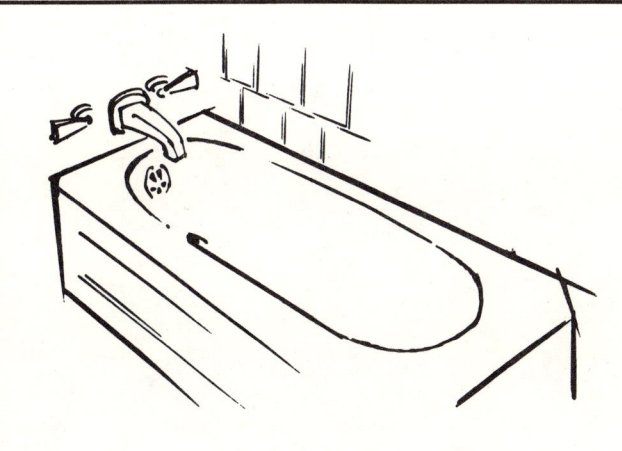

19. TUB

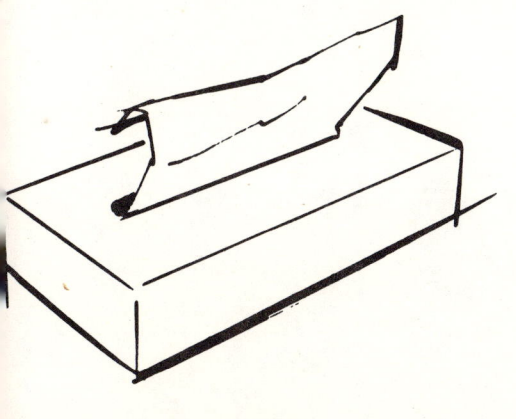

16. TISSUE

20. NOSE

The following exercise will illustrate the working application of our system called Visual Keys.

You are going to remember the following shopping list in perfect sequence. To associate these words with your Visual Keys, they must be brought together with active associations using exaggeration by making your pictures out of proportion, clearly visualizing your associations within your own mind's eye, or imagination. Again, the imagination is a mental picture which you form in your mind of something which is not actually in front of you at that particular moment.

Study the following illustrations from *1* to *10*, for a period of three minutes. These illustrations are suggestions of what you might visualize if the objects were presented in printed form only.

EXERCISE: MEMORIZE A SHOPPING LIST

1. HUT—Loaf of Bread

    See a huge loaf of bread leaning against the hut.

2. HEN—Whiskey

    See the hen drinking the whiskey, or sitting on top of the bottle.

3. HAM—Carrots

    See the carrots piercing the ham.

4. HARE—Pretzels

    Visualize the hare munching pretzels... pretzels on his ears, all around him.

EXERCISE: MEMORIZE A SHOPPING LIST

5. **HILL—Pickles**

   Picture huge pickles rolling down the hill.

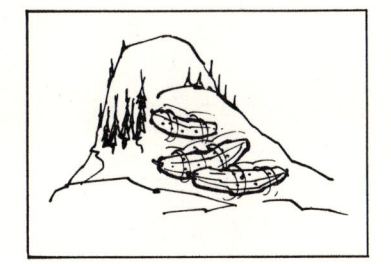

6. **JAY—Tomatoes**

   See the jay pecking at the tomato.

7. **HOOK—Donuts**

   Visualize the donuts on the hook.

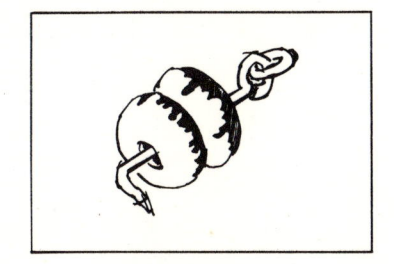

8. **HIVE—Paper Cups**

   See the hive crammed into a paper cup.

9. **APE—Playing Cards**

   See the ape throwing playing cards into the air.

10. **TOES—Apple Pie**

    Get yourself into the act! Wiggle your toes in an apple pie.

Now You Try It!

The next five items on your shopping list will be tied to your Visual Keys from *11* to *15*. Remember to use your imagination and bring the objects together through active association.

VISUAL KEYS	ASSOCIATION	GROCERY ITEM
11. TIDE		Apples and Oranges
12. TIN		Mustard
13. TAM		Cigarettes
14. TIRE		Potato Chips
15. TAIL		3 One Pound T-Bone Steaks

Test Yourself

Write the list of items you have memorized next to the Visual Key Words below.

1. HUT _____   9. APE _____
2. HEN _____   10. TOES _____
3. HAM _____   11. TIDE _____
4. HARE _____   12. TIN _____
5. HILL _____   13. TAM _____
6. JAY _____   14. TIRE _____
7. HOOK _____   15. TAIL _____
8. HIVE _____

NUMBER CORRECT _____

You should have felt the stimulus of the associations coming back to mind each time you thought of one of the Key Words.

LET'S LEARN A SYSTEM 59

Exercise: Translate Words Into Numbers

You will become familiar with the Numerical Alphabet and all the letters that represent the numbers by translating words into numbers. After some practice you will be able to translate words into numbers quickly and easily.

Practice by translating the following list of words into numbers according to the way they sound. You may refer back to the Numerical Alphabet if necessary. It is recommended that you make a copy of the Numerical Alphabet on a 3 x 5 index card or on a small sheet of paper for easy reference.

PRINT	_____	PASTE	_____
JERSEY	_____	CARD	_____
GARAGE	_____	ENOUGH	_____
VACATION	_____	CAMERA	_____
CHALK	_____	BAR	_____
RAIL	_____	LAMB	_____
BAND	_____	JOURNAL	_____
HIGH	_____	KITCHEN	_____
CONCENTRATION	_____	GREAT	_____
NICHE	_____	FRESH	_____
PHILOSOPHY	_____	PNEUMONIA	_____
BANJO	_____	HORIZON	_____
THERMOMETER	_____	JUDGE	_____
LIGHT	_____	POPULAR	_____
TRICK	_____	FIDDLE	_____
LETTER	_____	BALLET	_____

ANSWERS TO EXERCISE

The following is the list of words which you translated into numbers.

LET'S LEARN A SYSTEM

The correct number is written next to each word. Check your numbers with the ones below to see how many words you translated correctly.

WORD	SOUND	NUMBER	WORD	SOUND	NUMBER
PRINT		9421	PASTE		901
JERSEY		640	CARD	(kard)	741
GARAGE	(garaje)	746	ENOUGH	(enuf)	28
VACATION	(vakashun)	8762	CAMERA	(kamera)	734
CHALK	(chak)	67	BAR		94
RAIL		45	LAMB	(lam)	53
BAND		921	JOURNAL		6425
HIGH	(hi)		KITCHEN	(kichen)	762
CONCEN-TRATION	(konsentrashun)	72021462	GREAT		741
NICHE		26	FRESH		846
PHILOSO-PHY	(filosofy)	8508	PNEU-MONIA	(numonia)	232
BANJO		926	HORIZON		402
THERMOM-ETER		143314	JUDGE	(juj)	66
LIGHT	(lite)	51	POPULAR		9954
TRICK	(trik)	147	FIDDLE	(fidle)	815
LETTER	(leter)	514	BALLET	(balay)	95

After you have completed and checked your list, practice translating additional words wherever you may be. As an example, when you sit down to have a cup of coffee. Look up and say—ah! Cup—7–9. Coffee—7–8. Floor—8–5–4. Chair—6–4. Suit—0–1. Shirt—6–4–1. There are thousands of words all around you to translate into numbers. You will never run out of them. Practice a few moments each day. Soon you will know the Numerical Alphabet thoroughly and you will be able to translate words into numbers quickly and with ease.

HOW TO APPLY THE SYSTEM

Chapter **Five**

In the preceding chapter, we learned a system for giving words numerical value. We also learned that these words are a part of a system called Visual Keys. The first 20 words in this system were introduced and applied to remember the shopping list.

In this system, we will reach a total of 100 Visual Key Words. We suggest that you learn these words in groups of 20. As we learn our next group of Visual Key Words, we will also apply them in a practical way by associating facts with them.

21. NET
24. NERO
27. NECK
22. NUN
25. NAIL
28. NAVY
23. NAME
26. NICHE
29. KNOB

Visual Key Words 21–30

30. MICE

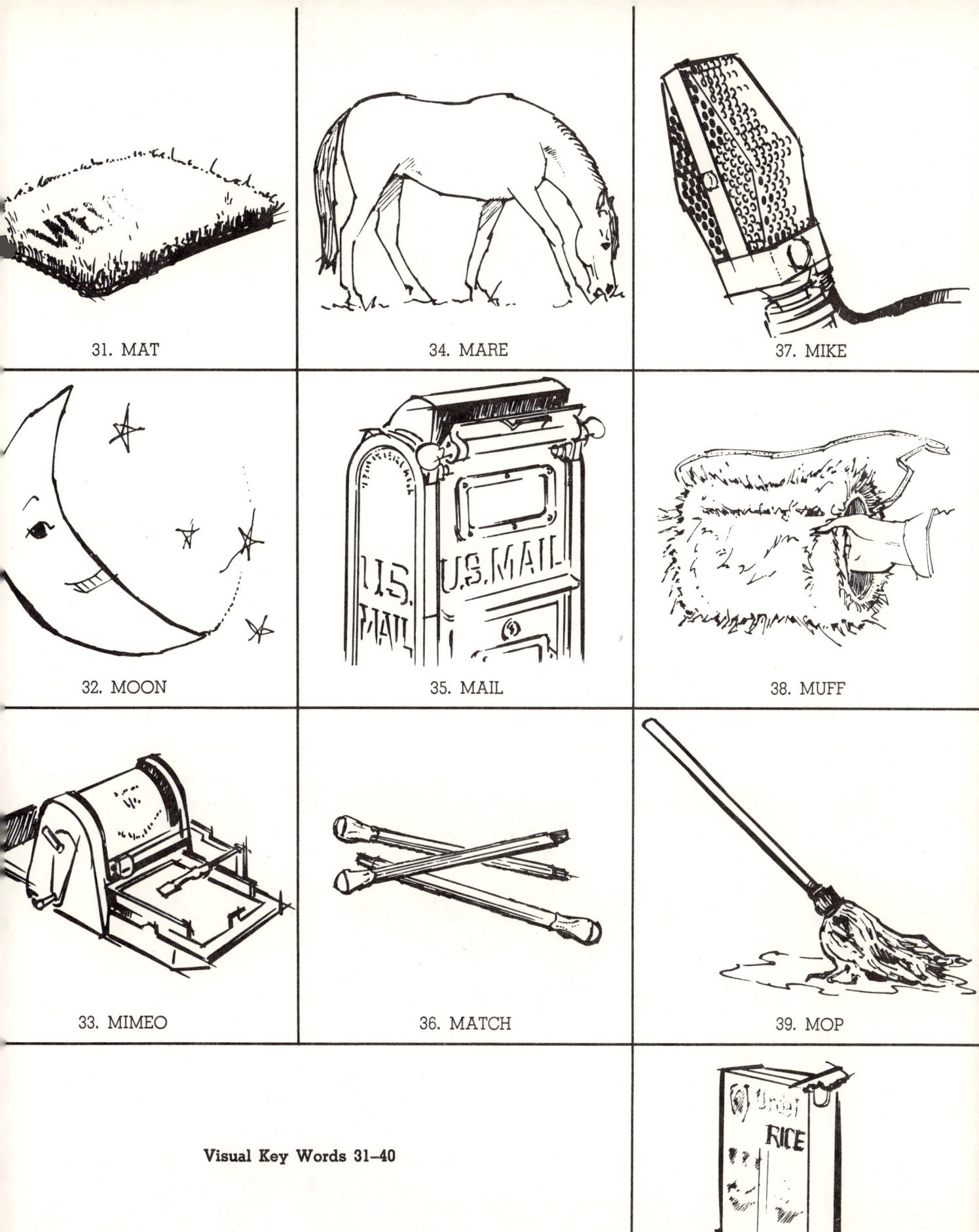

31. MAT
34. MARE
37. MIKE
32. MOON
35. MAIL
38. MUFF
33. MIMEO
36. MATCH
39. MOP

Visual Key Words 31–40

40. RICE

Let us suppose that you are the chairman of a discussion group. Tomorrow at 10:00 A.M., you are going to lead a discussion on book titles of 20 best sellers that have sold over two million copies. Everyone at the table will have a printed copy of the list. You want to make sure that as group leader you conduct the meeting as an expert. You want to have all these book titles keyed to memory so that you will not need to refer to the printed list.

As the expert you would not only want to know all of them, but be able to refer to them both in sequence and out of sequence as well. By applying the Visual Key method this can be accomplished easily.

We will use our Visual Key Words beginning with number *21*. The reason we are not beginning with *1* is because we should get into the habit of using the higher Keys as well as the lower ones.

By using *21-40* as a form of classification you can refer back to *21* as your beginning title and pick out the titles both in and out of sequence.

The *1* in *21* will represent the first book, the second *2* in *22* represents the second book and the *3* in *23* represents the third book. Likewise, the *1* in *31* signifies the *11th* book. It is not necessary to always go back to Key Word number *1*: HUT. Get into the habit of applying your higher Visual Keys. By continual use they will become more symbolic and easier to apply.

Our Visual Key Word for *21* is NET. The book title is "Alice In Wonderland."

> Picture Alice (whatever she looks like to you) with her long blonde hair, holding a NET and running through the forest—or Alice could be falling into a NET. Concentrate on visualizing Alice and the NET for five seconds. NET and "Alice in Wonderland."

HOW TO APPLY THE SYSTEM

Our Key Word for *22* is NUN. The book title is "Ben Hur."

We can take something from within the book itself to associate to the Key Word. As an example—part of the theme in the book "Ben Hur" is chariot racing. Use your imagination and picture the NUN boarding the chariot and saying, "Move over, I'm taking over!" Think of the NUN and the chariot will come to mind. The chariot symbolizes the book "Ben Hur." NUN and "Ben Hur."

Our Visual Key Word for *23* is NAME. The book title is "Christmas Carol."

To represent CHRISTMAS you can visualize a Christmas tree. Since Carol is a name, you can visualize a huge NAME plate with the name Carol on it. You can visualize a Christmas tree with name plates decorating it. And the name on the name plate? Of course! Carol. Or if you prefer you can picture a Christmas tree to represent Christmas, and see carolers around the Christmas tree singing Carols. And of course they are all holding huge name plates. NAME and "Christmas Carol."

The Key Word for *24* is NERO. The book title is "Gone With The Wind."

This one is easy, for you can visualize NERO fiddling while Rome burns. See the wind fanning the flames. The cue WIND will remind you of "Gone With The Wind." Or, if you prefer, see NERO burning Rome—then burning the city of Atlanta, a scene from the book, "Gone With The Wind." NERO and "Gone With The Wind."

The Key Word for *25* is NAIL. The book title is "How To Win Friends and Influence People."

Now you must make a positive association. Visualize yourself presenting your friend with a solid gold NAIL, trying to win him and influence him. Or, if you have a mental picture of the book (perhaps the paperback edition), then you can see yourself NAILing the book to your wall. NAIL and "How To Win Friends and Influence People."

The Key Word for *26* is NICHE. The book title is "In His Steps."

Now picture a NICHE with steps leading to it, and someone walking up into the NICHE—in his steps. NICHE and "In His Steps."

The Key Word for *27* is NECK. We will associate two book titles with this Key Word, "Ishmael" and the sequel, "Self Raised."

This association will bring back both titles. You may see the Biblical character Ishmael leading the giraffe by the NECK across the desert and being self-raised. If you are not familiar with the Biblical character, then use your imagination and take the sound of the name Ishmael and make familiar words from it. See the giraffe having lunch and dipping his NECK down to eat a bowl of FISH MEAL (fish meal sounds like Ishmael). And then after he finishes, his NECK is self-raised. NECK and "Ishmael," and the sequel, "Self Raised."

These associations are suggestions for the way in which you can memorize the first seven book titles. For the remainder of the list, make your own associations. Remember to make a strong visual image and use your imagination! The more active and imaginative the mental picture, the faster will be your recall, and the more lasting the retention you will have of these facts.

Memorize 20 Book Titles

VISUAL KEY WORD	BOOK TITLE	ASSOCIATION
21. NET	"Alice in Wonderland"	_____
22. NUN	"Ben Hur"	_____
23. NAME	"Christmas Carol"	_____
24. NERO	"Gone with the Wind"	_____
25. NAIL	"How To Win Friends and Influence People"	_____
26. NICHE	"In His Steps"	_____
27. NECK	"Ishmael," "Self Raised"	_____
28. NAVY	"Ivanhoe"	_____
29. KNOB	"Last of the Mohicans"	_____
30. MICE	"Little Women"	_____

HOW TO APPLY THE SYSTEM   67

| VISUAL KEY WORD | BOOK TITLE | ASSOCIATION |

31. MAT   "Mother Goose"   _____
32. MOON   "One World"   _____
33. MIMEO   "Plays of Shakespeare"   _____
34. MARE   "The Robe"   _____
35. MAIL   "Robinson Crusoe"   _____
36. MATCH   "See Here, Private
                  Hargrove"   _____
37. MIKE   "Stories of the Bible"   _____
38. MUFF   "Tom Sawyer"   _____
39. MOP   "Treasure Island"   _____

VISUAL KEY WORD	BOOK TITLE	ASSOCIATION
40. RICE	"A Tree Grows in Brooklyn"	_____

Now list the titles on a sheet of paper, let's check to see how many of these you remember correctly.

Test Yourself

Your list of Visual Key Words is found below. Visualize each Key Word again and your association to represent the book title should appear with it. Then write down the title of the book on the line next to the Key Word. Should you find that you have a weak association on one of your Key Words, don't stop and ponder over it. Continue and when you have finished the entire list, go back and think about it. Ask yourself, what did I do with it? Who was in the picture with it? Where was it located? What? and Why? This reasoning factor should stimulate the association and bring the book title back to mind.

VISUAL KEY WORD	BOOK TITLE
21. NET	_____
22. NUN	_____
23. NAME	_____
24. NERO	_____
25. NAIL	_____
26. NICHE	_____
27. NECK	_____
28. NAVY	_____
29. KNOB	_____
30. MICE	_____
31. MAT	_____
32. MOON	_____
33. MIMEO	_____
34. MARE	_____
35. MAIL	_____
36. MATCH	_____
37. MIKE	_____

HOW TO APPLY THE SYSTEM 69

VISUAL KEY WORD   BOOK TITLE

   38. MUFF   _____
   39. MOP   _____
   40. RICE   _____

                                              NUMBER CORRECT _____

Any association that did not come back to mind as you went through the test, you should check again on the original list. Then make a more active and vivid association to support and strengthen your original mental picture. Test yourself on this list of book titles within 24 hours and see how much you retain at that time. You should find that all 20 titles come back with ease.

At the beginning, it was mentioned that we can remember information associated with the Visual Key Words both in and out of sequence. Let's see how it works out of sequence. Write the name of the book title next to each Visual Key Word listed below.

VISUAL KEY WORD   BOOK TITLE

   30. MICE   _____
   22. NUN   _____
   23. NAME   _____
   28. NAVY   _____
   32. MOON   _____
   35. MAIL   _____
   39. MOP   _____
   21. NET   _____
   29. KNOB   _____
   40. RICE   _____
   37. MIKE   _____
   25. NAIL   _____
   33. MIMEO   _____

You see how easily material can be associated with your Visual Key Words. Any type of material can be associated in the same manner. On the following pages you will find illustrations of your next 40 Visual Key Words. Remember to learn them *only* 20 at a time. Then, at the end of the chapter, we will again apply these Key Words to lists of facts and ideas.

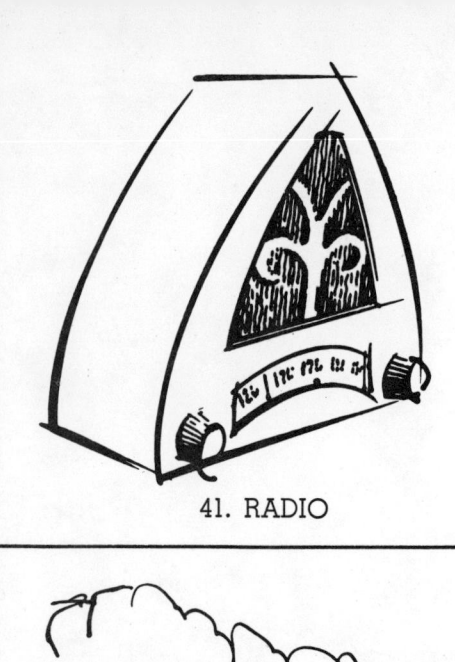

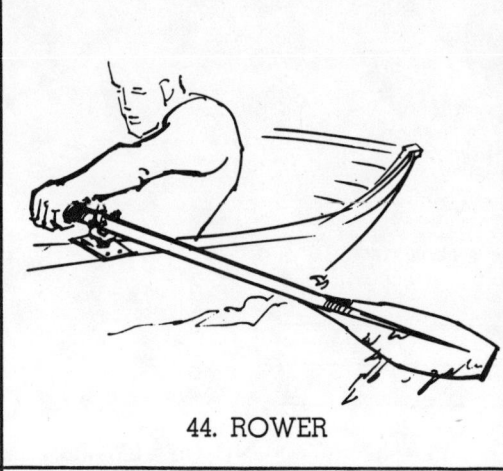

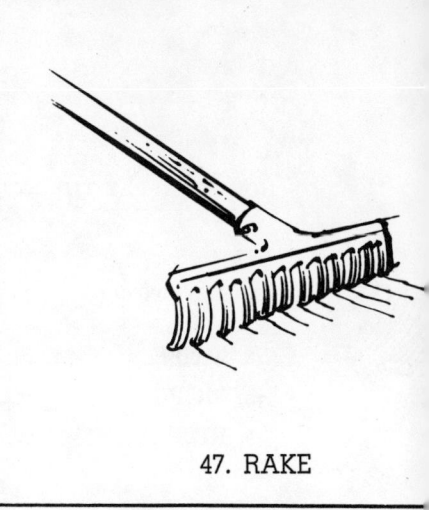

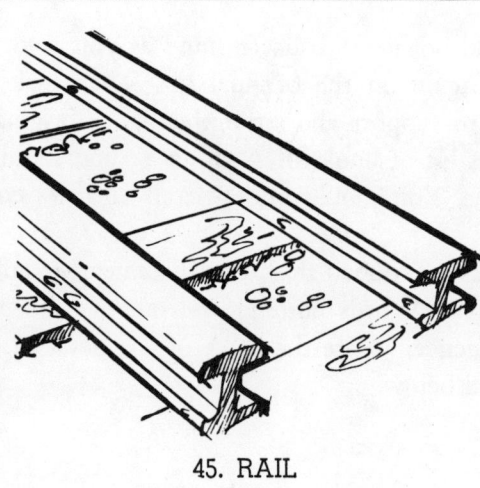

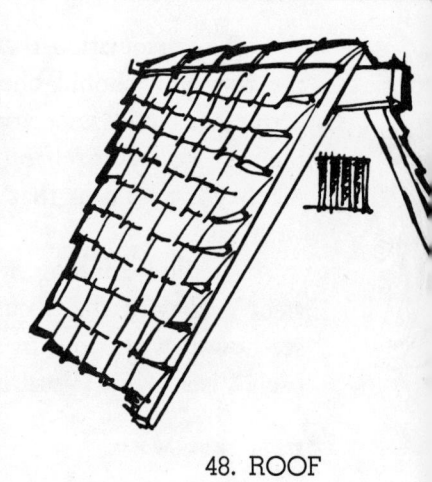

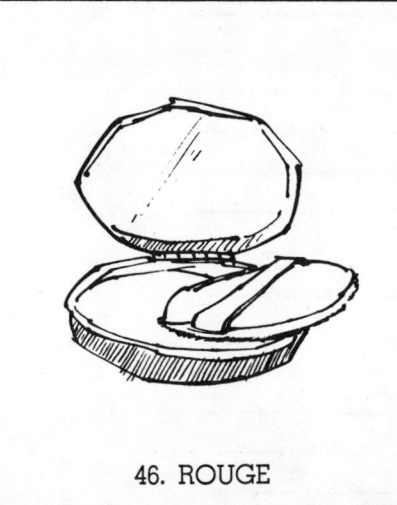

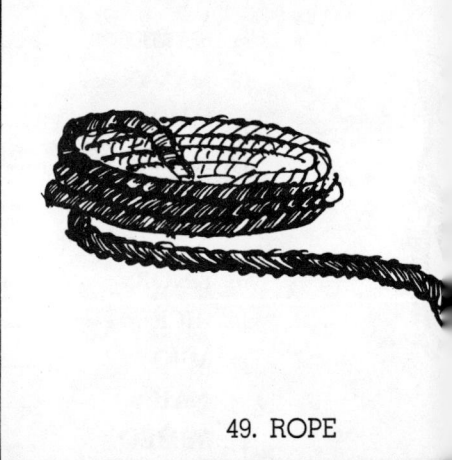

41. RADIO
44. ROWER
47. RAKE
42. RAIN
45. RAIL
48. ROOF
43. RAM
46. ROUGE
49. ROPE

Visual Key Words 41-50

50. LACE

51. LIGHT

54. LAIR

57. LAKE

52. LION

55. LILY

58. LOAF

53. LAMB

56. LASH

59. L.P.

Visual Key Words 51–60

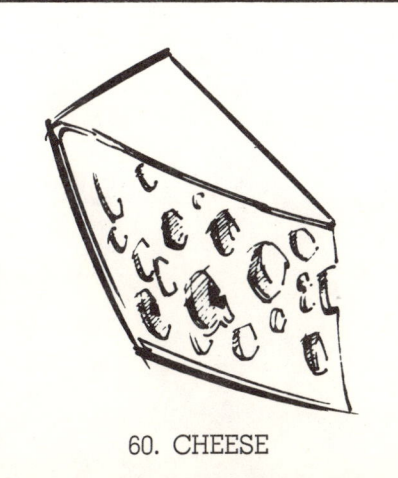

60. CHEESE

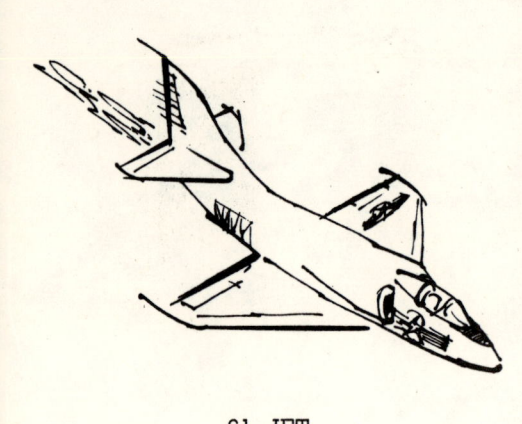

61. JET

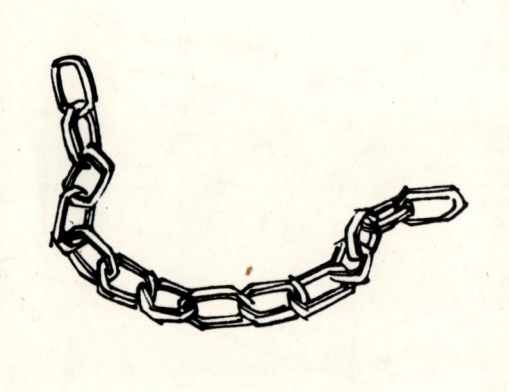

62. CHAIN

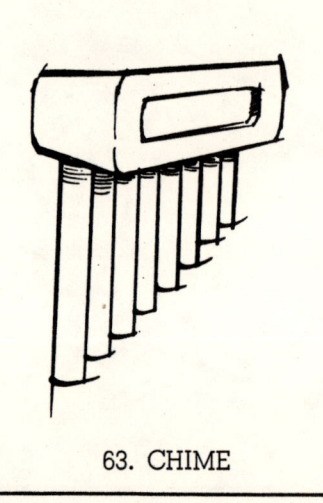

63. CHIME

64. CHAIR

65. JELLY

66. JUDGE

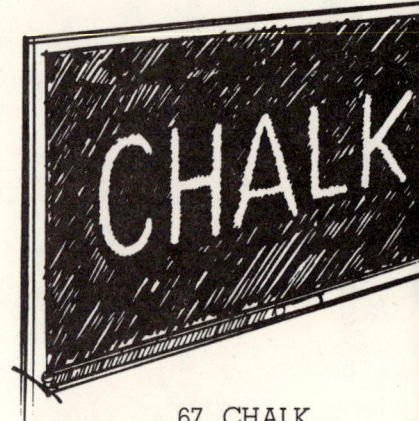

67. CHALK

68. CHIEF

69. CHOP

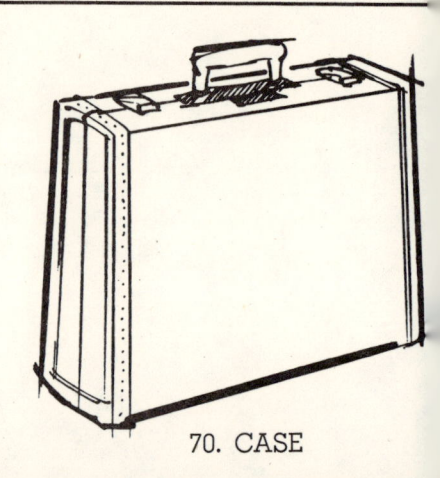

70. CASE

Visual Key Words 61–70

72

71. CAT

74. CAR

77. CAKE

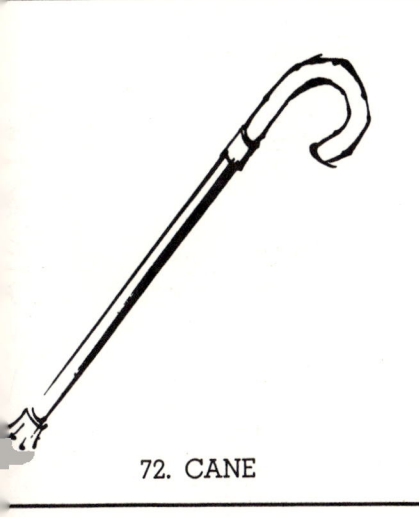

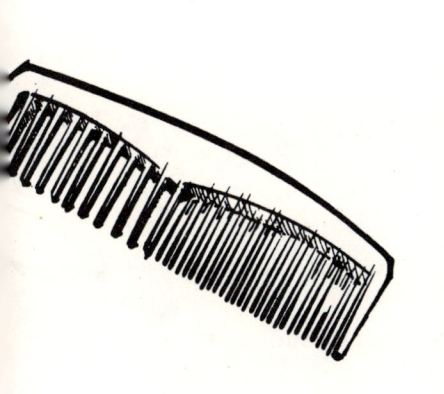

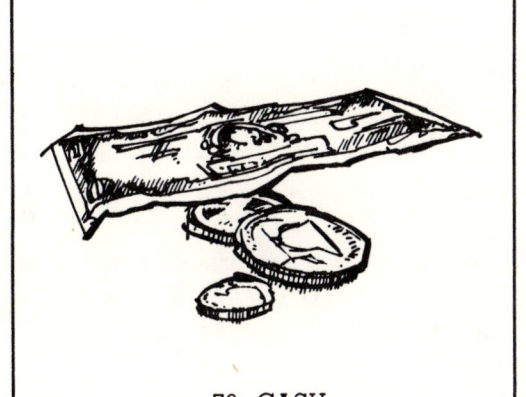

72. CANE

75. COAL

78. COFFEE

73. COMB

76. CASH

79. CAPE

Visual Key Words 71–80

73

80. FUSE

When you have mastered these 80 Visual Key Words, then you are ready for actual, practical application. On the following pages, you are given an exercise to assist you in becoming familiar with the Visual Key Words. Although this is just an exercise, the information you are associating will be useful. Practice the exercise that is given, then you will find it easy to apply this numerical system later in the book to historical dates, telephone numbers and numerical data of all types.

PRACTICE EXERCISE

Let's practice the application of our Visual Key Words by memorizing the books of the Bible, King James Version. Even though you may not use the King James Version, practice this exercise and then apply the same principles to memorize the books of your own version.

The King James Version of the Holy Bible is separated into two parts—the Old Testament and the New Testament. Since there are 39 books in the Old Testament, we will use our Visual Key Words from 1–39 to associate these books in our mind. There are 27 books in the New Testament, so we will use our Visual Key Words from 51–77 for this exercise. We begin the New Testament with our Key Word 51 to keep the two separated—to know where one Testament ends and the other begins. In this way, they are automatically classified. Ready to begin? *Say Yes!!*

Books of the Bible:
  Old Testament

The first Book in the Old Testament is Genesis. Genesis is not a word that you can readily picture. We can substitute the word "genie," which sounds similar and can be pictured. When we think of "genie" again, the sound will remind us of Genesis. Since HUT is number *1* on our Visual Key Word list, we want to bring the HUT and GENIE together. See the GENIE leaning against the HUT; use your imagination and visualize as illustrated. HUT–GENESIS.

HOW TO APPLY THE SYSTEM 75

Exodus, the second Book, is tied to HEN, our Visual Key Word for number 2. To remember the book of EXODUS, we can substitute "exit," which sounds similar and will remind us of EXODUS when we think of the word "exit" again. Notice the illustration. HEN–EXODUS.

Leviticus, the third Book, is tied to HAM. To represent the name LEVITICUS, we can think of "Levi's," a type of denim pants. You can picture the HAM stuffed into a pair of LEVI's. HAM–LEVITICUS.

Numbers is the fourth Book, and is associated to HARE, our fourth Visual Key Word. Visualize NUMBERS all over the HARE. HARE–NUMBERS.

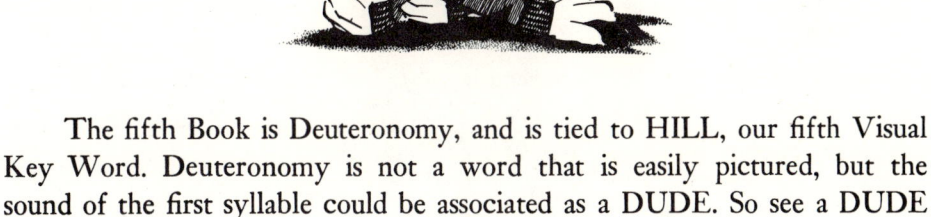

The fifth Book is Deuteronomy, and is tied to HILL, our fifth Visual Key Word. Deuteronomy is not a word that is easily pictured, but the sound of the first syllable could be associated as a DUDE. So see a DUDE at the bottom of the HILL. When you think of DUDE, the sound will remind you that it is the first syllable of the Book of Deuteronomy. **HILL-DEUTERONOMY** or (see a dude running after me down the hill.)

Now you're on your own. Associate the remainder of the Books of the Old Testament in the same manner. Substitute wherever necessary by the sound of the word and then make a vivid mental picture of the Key Word and the name of the Book going together. Write your associations in the spaces provided.

VISUAL KEY WORD	BOOK	ASSOCIATION
6. JAY	Joshua	_____
7. HOOK	Judges	_____
8. HIVE	Ruth	_____
9. APE	I Samuel	_____
10. TOES	II Samuel	_____
11. TIDE	I Kings	_____
12. TIN	II Kings	_____
13. TAM	I Chronicles	_____
14. TIRE	II Chronicles	_____
15. TAIL	Ezra	_____
16. TISSUE	Nehemiah	_____
17. TAG	Esther	_____
18. TAFFY	Job	_____
19. TUB	Psalms	_____

HOW TO APPLY THE SYSTEM 77

VISUAL KEY WORD	BOOK	ASSOCIATION
20. NOSE	Proverbs	_____
21. NET	Ecclesiastes	_____
22. NUN	Song of Solomon	_____
23. NAME	Isaiah	_____
24. NERO	Jeremiah	_____
25. NAIL	Lamentations	_____
26. NICHE	Ezekiel	_____
27. NECK	Daniel	_____
28. NAVY	Hosea	_____
29. KNOB	Joel	_____
30. MICE	Amos	_____
31. MAT	Obadiah	_____
32. MOON	Jonah	_____
33. MIMEO	Micah	_____
34. MARE	Nahum	_____
35. MAIL	Habakkuk	_____
36. MATCH	Zephaniah	_____
37. MIKE	Haggai	_____
38. MUFF	Zechariah	_____
39. MOP	Malachi	_____

Test Yourself

To check your retention of the material which you have just learned, write the Book of the Old Testament which was associated with the Visual Key Words below.

VISUAL KEY WORD	BOOK OF OLD TESTAMENT
1. HUT	_____
2. HEN	_____
3. HAM	_____
4. HARE	_____
5. HILL	_____
6. JAY	_____
7. HOOK	_____

VISUAL KEY WORD	BOOK OF OLD TESTAMENT
8. HIVE	_____
9. APE	_____
10. TOES	_____
11. TIDE	_____
12. TIN	_____
13. TAM	_____
14. TIRE	_____
15. TAIL	_____
16. TISSUE	_____
17. TAG	_____
18. TAFFY	_____
19. TUB	_____
20. NOSE	_____
21. NET	_____
22. NUN	_____
23. NAME	_____
24. NERO	_____
25. NAIL	_____
26. NICHE	_____
27. NECK	_____
28. NAVY	_____
29. KNOB	_____
30. MICE	_____
31. MAT	_____
32. MOON	_____
33. MIMEO	_____
34. MARE	_____
35. MAIL	_____
36. MATCH	_____
37. MIKE	_____
38. MUFF	_____
39. MOP	_____

Your Score _____

HOW TO APPLY THE SYSTEM 79

Books of the New Testament

To associate the Books of the New Testament in their numerical order, we will begin with our Visual Key Word for 51. Remembering the starting point, Key Word 51, gives a classification to the New Testament. Associate each Book in the same manner as you memorized the Books of the Old Testament, then test your retention.

51. LIGHT–Matthew

We can visualize our Key Word LIGHT screwed into a MATH book. MATH to represent MATTHEW. LIGHT–MATTHEW.

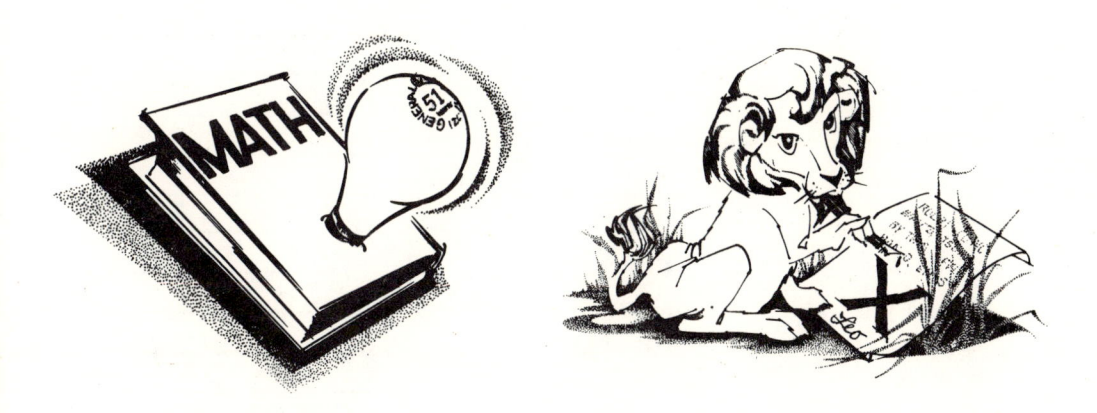

52. LION–Mark

We can visualize our Key Word LION making his MARK on a paper. You know, X *marks* the spot. LION–MARK.

53. LAMB–Luke

See our LAMB testing a pan of water to see if it is still LUKEwarm. LUKEWARM for Luke and LAMB. LAMB–LUKE.

Now, you're on your own. Use your imagination and associate each Visual Key Word with the name of the Book of the New Testament in an active, visual way. Write your associations in the spaces provided.

VISUAL KEY WORD	BOOK	ASSOCIATION
54. LAIR	John	_____
55. LILY	Acts	_____
56. LASH	Romans	_____
57. LAKE	I Corinthians	_____

VISUAL KEY WORD	BOOK	ASSOCIATION
58. LOAF	II Corinthians	_____
59. L.P.	Galatians	_____
60. CHEESE	Ephesians	_____
61. JET	Philippians	_____
62. CHAIN	Colossians	_____
63. CHIME	I Thessalonians	_____
64. CHAIR	II Thessalonians	_____
65. JELLY	I Timothy	_____
66. JUDGE	II Timothy	_____
67. CHALK	Titus	_____
68. CHIEF	Philemon	_____
69. CHOP	Hebrews	_____
70. CASE	James	_____
71. CAT	I Peter	_____
72. CANE	II Peter	_____
73. COMB	I John	_____
74. CAR	II John	_____
75. COAL	III John	_____
76. CASH	Jude	_____
77. CAKE	Revelation	_____

Now that you have associated all the Books of the New Testament, take a test of your retention of this information.

Test Yourself

Check your retention of the Books of the New Testament. On the line provided beside each Visual Key Word below, write the name of the Book that was associated with it.

VISUAL KEY WORD	BOOK OF NEW TESTAMENT
51. LIGHT	_____
52. LION	_____
53. LAMB	_____

HOW TO APPLY THE SYSTEM

VISUAL KEY WORD	BOOK OF NEW TESTAMENT
54. LAIR	_____
55. LILY	_____
56. LASH	_____
57. LAKE	_____
58. LOAF	_____
59. L.P.	_____
60. CHEESE	_____
61. JET	_____
62. CHAIN	_____
63. CHIME	_____
64. CHAIR	_____
65. JELLY	_____
66. JUDGE	_____
67. CHALK	_____
68. CHIEF	_____
69. CHOP	_____
70. CASE	_____
71. CAT	_____
72. CANE	_____
73. COMB	_____
74. CAR	_____
75. COAL	_____
76. CASH	_____
77. CAKE	_____

YOUR SCORE _____

Students who complete this exercise come to me and exclaim that they could have spent a great deal of energy attempting to remember the Books of the Old and New Testament. Now, with this technique, they not only know them in their correct sequence, like an expert, but can call them out of sequence as well!

In the following chapter, you will find your Key Words from 81–100. Study these Words and you will have your complete Visual Key Word System from 1–100.

You should apply all of your Visual Key Words at every opportunity. The system serves as an excellent classification of material and gives you a check list to make certain that all the material you need will be at your fingertips when you need it. You will have no doubt about your memory once you have associated facts and ideas in your mind. When a concrete visual picture has been made to bring an idea or fact together with your Visual Key Words, you will never have to guess. You will know.

These Visual Key Words as well as the Numerical Alphabet will be used to great advantage in remembering numerical data of all types in later chapters. Once you have mastered this method, you will find numerous uses for it in your everyday life.

REMEMBER ISOLATED FACTS

Chapter **Six**

Have you ever forgotten to return a telephone call to a friend or client? How many times have you failed to pick up the cleaning on your way home, or forgotten to mail an important letter? Have you ever entered your car to find that you had left your keys in another suit or were halfway to the office and had to go back for your briefcase?

Why do we seem to forget such simple things? To begin with, we all follow some daily routine. By constant repetition of certain activities they become second nature to us. We have overlearned them to such a degree that they have become a habit and require little conscious thinking. Actually, this doing-by-habit is very beneficial. It eliminates repeated conscious thinking and planning for the same activity. We can get up in the morning, dress, eat and leave for work without giving these matters much thought. What happens when we have to interrupt this routine?

Interruption of a routine calls for directing the mind away from that routine long enough to concentrate on the act of doing another task. We call this *Isolated Facts* to be remembered. With practice you can learn to remember Isolated Facts easily.

If you forget Isolated Facts, do not be too critical of yourself. True, it may be very inconvenient and you may say, "That was a stupid thing to do!" But this kind of forgetting is not indicative of your basic intelligence; rather it indicates mental habits. You simply did not pause to *think* and *associate* in the middle of a *routine situation* when a new thought was needed. You have heard many stories about the absent-minded professor. We do not doubt *his* intelligence, and you certainly should never doubt yours!

There are techniques you can apply to remember these Isolated Facts. Mainly we need a reminder that will trigger the memory at the right time. Practice the methods given in this chapter and you will find that it's easy to remember the little tasks as well as the big ones! If you have a technique that you have been applying, continue to do so. If a friend tells you of a technique that works for him, try it! If it works for you, use it!

Don't be in a hurry. Slow down. Haste will often cause a person to forget something he has to do. Tension will also misdirect the individual's mind in another direction. So relax and concentrate on these little tasks to be remembered.

Bring Home the Groceries

To remember to stop at the grocery store on your way home after work, choose a familiar object as a basic association and visualize the grocery items on it. A good object for this association is your car. When you need groceries, spend a few seconds building a strong mental picture of grocery items spread all over the hood of your car. When next you get into your car, there is the hood, stacked with groceries, in your imagination, of course! (Don't worry! They won't obstruct your view!)

When you have fulfilled your errand, the grocery items will disappear, leaving your hood clear to act as a reminder again.

Communicate with Others

One of my students decided to aid her husband who was notorious for leaving his briefcase at home. Many times during the period of a month he would call her on the phone and request that she bring the forgotten briefcase down to his office. The solution, she thought, was to place the briefcase by the front door . . . he couldn't miss it! That next morning, she did place his briefcase by the door. As he ran towards the door in his usual haste, he tripped over the case, kicked it aside, shouted, "Who put that there?" and then off he went!

When you apply a memory technique such as this one, tell everyone who is concerned what the purpose is and how the memory technique is to be applied!

PLAN AHEAD! To avoid forgetting a briefcase, dry cleaning, laundry or other items that should be taken with you when you leave your house, put them where you cannot miss seeing them.

Let's See Now . . . Where Did I Park My Car?

The scene: Miami, Florida. The Orange Bowl, Friday evening football game.

A group of college students went to the football game, arriving a few minutes after the game had started. They found that all the parking spaces near the Bowl were filled. Homeowners in the neighborhood were renting parking space on their lawns and backyards. After 10 minutes of circling the area, the students saw a lady signal to them to park in her yard. Hurriedly parking, the group of students dashed off to the game.

At 10 p.m., the game was over. Everyone proceeded to their car and drove off. This one group of students looked and looked for their car. They asked each other, "Was it this street or that street?" None of them had consciously observed a landmark, street address, cross street or description of the house where they had parked. An hour later, after continuous door bell ringing, they came upon the correct house. Embarrassing? Yes! And an exasperating waste of time.

So, to remember where you parked your car, always look for the nearest landmark, street names, cross streets or the aisle number in a parking lot. Don't look at the car in front of yours because by the time you return that car may be replaced by another one. Today many large parking areas are color-coded to jog your memory. You may be parked in the green lot or blue lot. Watch it!

Haste makes waste! Slow down and take that one moment to fix the association in mind.

Looking for Your Pen

Valuable time is lost looking for items such as a fountain pen, book, eyeglasses, an important letter or bill that you know you saw just a few moments before. Sound familiar? Chances are you put the item down hurriedly and rushed away! Spend a few seconds when you put the item down and notice the relationship between the item itself and the object on which it is placed. This method will save the time and frustration of going from room to room trying to relocate it.

Jog Your Memory

Suppose you have placed a call, and the party is out but will return in an hour. You are leaving for lunch but promise to call again upon returning to your own office. To remember to call, leave yourself a reminder. Is the phone always in one place? Move it! Put it on a chair, in the center of your desk, turn the receiver upside down, or place a folded piece of paper under the receiver. At the same time, visualize yourself phoning that person.

When you return, the obvious misplacement will remind you of the phone, and the phone will remind you of the call.

Locked Out!

One morning our former housekeeper, in great haste, dashed out of her apartment and pressed the door latch, locking the door behind her. Within 10 seconds after this act it dawned upon her—key was inside! The price was $7.50 for the locksmith to open the door and one hour of time wasted. All she had to do to save $7.50 and one hour's time was *to stop at the front door for a few seconds to check for her key.*

Do I Have Everything?

When you leave your home or office, don't rush out of the door! Stop for a few seconds—five or ten seconds is usually enough. Think:

"Where am I going? Do I have everything with me that I should?"

Check for keys, wallet, pen, your bank book because you have to stop at the bank, library, etc. Are the lights out, windows closed, heaters off? Then off you go! It is wiser to spend 10 seconds at the door, thinking, than 30 minutes on the return trip for that item left behind. Invest time . . . save time.

Forget-Me-Not

Have a place by your front door, such as a shelf or table, to put items you wish to take with you when you leave your home or office. At any time during the day that you think of an item which must go with you, take the time to put it on the shelf. As you go past the front door later, stop, clear the shelf, then off you go!

Where Is My Car?

One of my students told me of his friend who had the habit of going to work each day on the bus. One rainy morning he decided to take his own automobile. He parked it in a parking lot convenient to his office. By that afternoon the rain had stopped. After work, in his routine fashion, he boarded the bus and read the evening paper on the way home. As he walked towards his home, the view of the driveway was enough to remind him: car—downtown parking lot. Frustrated, he about-faced and boarded the next bus downtown to retrieve his car.

This fellow should have placed his car keys or parking lot ticket in a conspicuous place to act as a continuous reminder—car today, bus tomorrow!

Have a Place for Everything

Have you ever left your house without fountain pen, wallet, car keys or lighter? Simple items are often overlooked because we are convinced we shall never forget them. Therefore, we do not really concentrate on them.

A mental check list habit is invaluable for small personal items. Be organized! Each item you use daily should have a special permanent place; keys in one pocket, change in another. Every morning touch each pocket to see that the items are there. Once the habit is formed it becomes automatic, taking only a few seconds. Those few seconds will eliminate a possible trip back for a forgotten item!

You can develop your own techniques for remembering those little tasks that come up so unexpectedly during your everyday life. Be aware of your surroundings and be observant of everything you need to accomplish.

Visual Key Words 81–100

Let's memorize the last 20 Key Words of our Visual Key System. Remember to recognize your Numerical Alphabet as the basis of these Key Words.

In our 81–90 series, notice that all the Keys start with the letter "F." Then each word has combinations of F–T for 81, F–N for 82, F–M for 83, F–R for 84, F–L for 85, F–SH for 86, F–G for 87, F–F for 88 and F–B for 89.

Our 91–100 series all begin with the letter "B." 91 combines the letters B and D, B–N for 92, B–M for 93, B–R for 94, B–L for 95, B–DG for 96, B–K for 97, B–F for 98, and B–B for 99. Number 100 combines D–S–S to make the word DAISIES. The following is a list of illustrations of the Visual Key Words from 81–100.

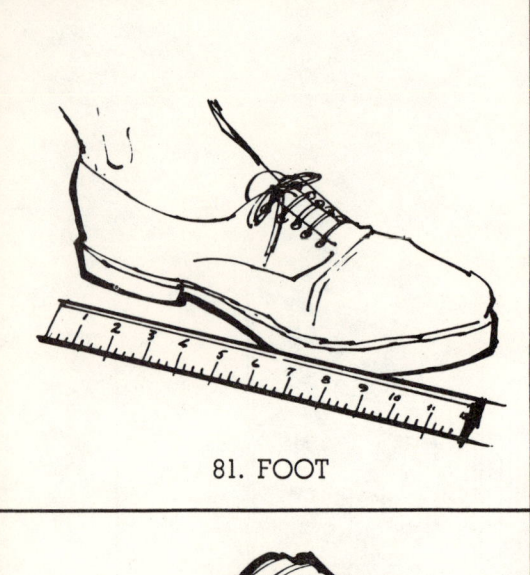

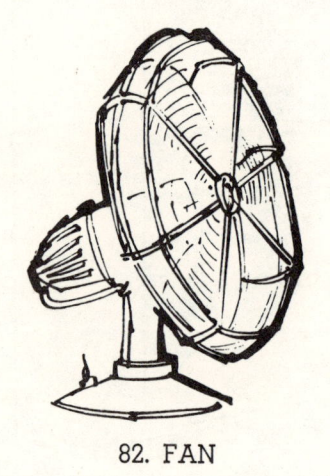

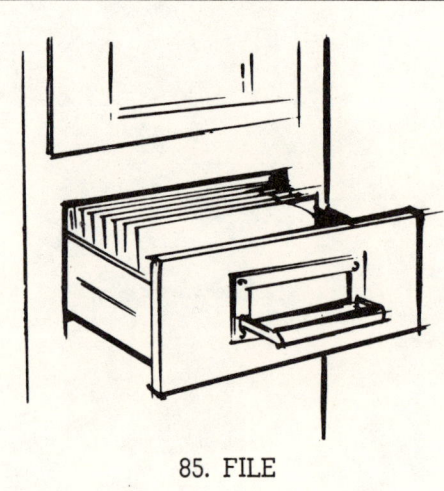

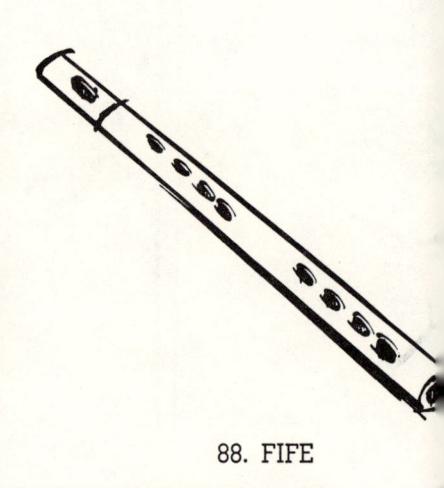

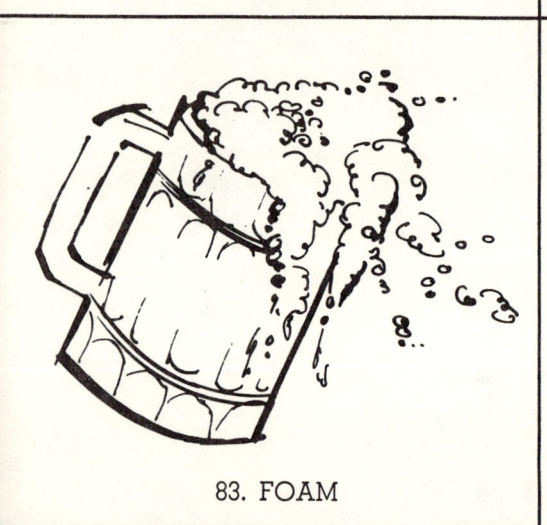

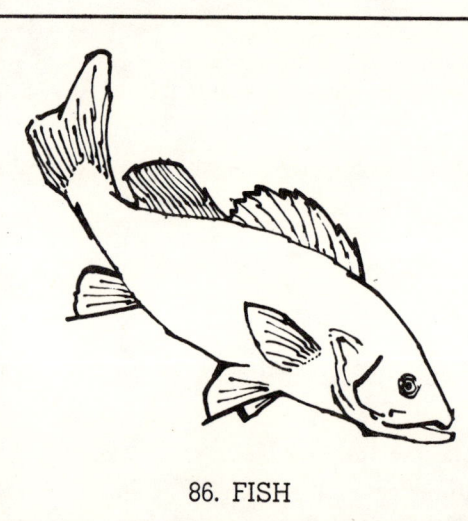

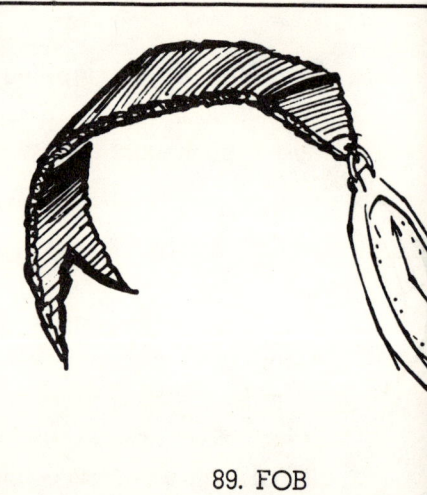

81. FOOT
84. FIRE
87. FIG
82. FAN
85. FILE
88. FIFE
83. FOAM
86. FISH
89. FOB

Visual Key Words 81–90

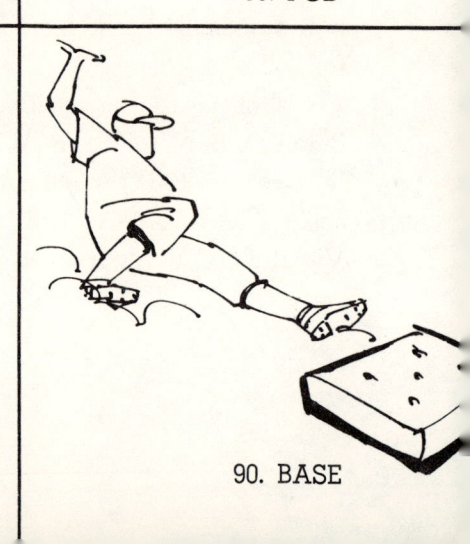

90. BASE

91. BED
94. BAR
97. BIKE 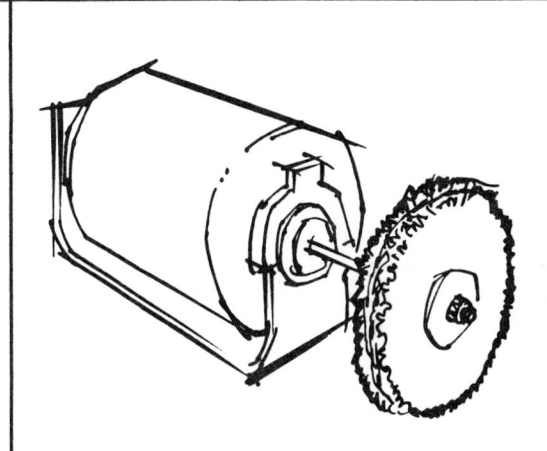
92. BONE
95. BALL
98. BUFF 
93. BOMB
96. BADGE
99. BABY
100. DAISIES

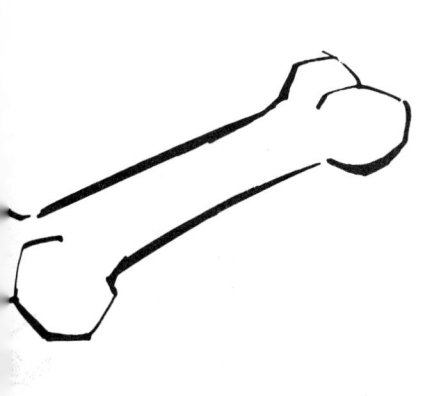

Visual Key Words 91–100

Before moving on to the next chapter, review all 100 Key Words and try to gain fluency in calling these Words from one to the other. Also, know them out of sequence as well, such as number 61–JET, number 71–CAT, number 64–CHAIR.

The following Review Chart lists, in a classified manner, your 100 Visual Key Words. Study this Chart and you will find it a valuable aid in reviewing and reinforcing Key Words in your mind.

Review Chart of Your 100 Visual Key Words

1. HUT	2. HEN	3. HAM	4. HARE	5. HILL	6. JAY	7. HOOK	8. HIVE	9. APE	10. TOES
11. TIDE	12. TIN	13. TAM	14. TIRE	15. TAIL	16. TISSUE	17. TAG	18. TAFFY	19. TUB	20. NOSE
21. NET	22. NUN	23. NAME	24. NERO	25. NAIL	26. NICHE	27. NECK	28. NAVY	29. KNOB	30. MICE
31. MAT	32. MOON	33. MIMEO	34. MARE	35. MAIL	36. MATCH	37. MIKE	38. MUFF	39. MOP	40. RICE
41. RADIO	42. RAIN	43. RAM	44. ROWER	45. RAIL	46. ROUGE	47. RAKE	48. ROOF	49. ROPE	50. LACE
51. LIGHT	52. LION	53. LAMB	54. LAIR	55. LILY	56. LASH	57. LAKE	58. LOAF	59. L.P.	60. CHEESE
61. JET	62. CHAIN	63. CHIME	64. CHAIR	65. JELLY	66. JUDGE	67. CHALK	68. CHIEF	69. CHOP	70. CASE
71. CAT	72. CANE	73. COMB	74. CAR	75. COAL	76. CASH	77. CAKE	78. COFFEE	79. CAPE	80. FUSE
81. FOOT	82. FAN	83. FOAM	84. FIRE	85. FILE	86. FISH	87. FIG	88. FIFE	89. FOB	90. BASE
91. BED	92. BONE	93. BOMB	94. BAR	95. BALL	96. BADGE	97. BIKE	98. BUFF	99. BABY	100. DAISIES

HOW TO REMEMBER
NAMES AND FACES

Chapter **Seven**

"If you'd like a formula for instant public relations, here it is: *remember people's names.*"

William J. Breen, Vice President of the Bank of America, offers this timely advice to all his employees. He realizes, as all businessmen do, that calling customers or clients by name is a most important business asset. It creates good will for the company and brings in business because everyone wants to be remembered as a person as well as a business prospect.

In all my years as a teacher of memory training, there has been one phase of remembering requested by all my students: the methods for remembering names and faces. They wish to avoid the necessity of lamenting, "The face is familiar, but I just can't remember the name!"

When you can remember names and faces, you become a more self-confident and poised individual. Many of my students have related to me how they have increased their income by remembering names and facts previously related to them by a customer and client. Some have built a fine reputation on their ability to remember names.

An excellent example of increase of business and income is cited by a former student, Bob Frederick. Bob is the owner of Frederick Cleaners in Los Angeles. He realizes that in business it is very important to remember clients and to call them by name.

When Bob completed my memory training course, he designed his new dry cleaning establishment so that he, as well as his employees at the call office counter, can see the customer as he drives in. While the customer is getting out of his car, the girls will go and get his clothing, have it and the receipt ready for him when he reaches the counter. Bob's business has doubled since moving into the new building and using this system. Bob also says that when he is writing up the invoice for the customer that he will remember the address as well as the name.

Bob also made a reputation for himself socially. One night at a charity organization dinner, he was introduced to 80 people as they came in the door. He had never met any of these individuals before. During the entertainment portion of the evening, Bob took the mike and astounded all present by announcing that he could call all 80 persons by name. He said that to raise additional money for this charity, every person whose name he called correctly should donate $1.00, and for each one he missed, *he* would donate $5.00!

The group agreed and he proceeded to call the names of all 80 persons without a single error!

Another example of the impression left by remembering names and faces was related to me by Mona Ling, a nationally known and respected telephone sales trainer. She wrote to me several months after completing my memory training course:

> Realizing how important it is to remember names of people, I worked on this phase of your training first. Also, as I meet about fifty

to one hundred persons every week, I have a great exposure to them. Sometimes, I meet two or three hundred people at one time at large sales workshops.

I can remember 22 names within about two minutes—or as fast as I can meet the people. The men are introduced to me by their first and last names. My programs are informal and we use first names so the managers make it a point to introduce the men by their first names or "nicknames." I find that it has been easier to train the men after a strong name association has been made. . . .

I trained the management of the companies first. This was done in three states and several cities. Then when I trained the agents of these men, many of their managers came back with their men. Though this was several weeks later, I recognized every manager by name and his strengths and weaknesses in selling.

In training from 12 to 24 men, I find that I can remember what the men say, how they say it, how they react, their manners of speech, shyness or aggressiveness in manner, nervousness, or poise, mannerisms, or anything else that might help or detract from making a sale or appointment. Many times these men call me several weeks or several months after the training program has been completed to ask a question about some problem or presentation. When I hear them speak, my mental pictures of the men come back . . . it did not work this way prior to working on memory. I can now train groups of 12 to 24 men in two six-hour sessions instead of three or four sessions, because my memory is keen and accurate. This has made my judgment more accurate. I train more rapidly, yet more accurately than ever before. . . .

My usual program is now two six-hour sessions. I might add that both of these sessions are given without referring to a note. I do on-the-spot analyses of the presentations which has speeded my training program considerably. . . .

Miss Ling leaves an indelible impression on everyone she meets and works with because of her ability to remember names, and important facts about these people. Of course her business has increased, and her memory has enabled her to speed up her program, and helps her to teach in a more relaxed manner. Now that she can remember her material and all the names, she can teach with keen concentration without having to think in the middle of a point, "I want to call on him, but what is his name?"

The ability to remember names is important to the student, also, because he must remember the names and faces surrounding the events in his textbooks. The techniques presented in these chapters on names and faces should be applied to the retention of names in the news, names and events in your textbooks, names of the people you meet every day, names of authors and books which you wish to remember. Every day you have a need to remember names. A name may be needed at a moment's notice.

You should realize that the same basic techniques are used to remember any name, no matter what the necessary surrounding information may be.

Remembering names and faces is easy, once you know how. Give this a little thought and you'll agree that these two words are the secret to anything—*know how!*

First, pay attention to the name. Listen, and you are already on your way. Be assured that the ability to remember names and faces is not necessarily a gift. It is a faculty that *you*, too, can develop.

On the following pages are the Six Secrets to Success in remembering names. Master them and use them in your everyday life, and you will find that remembering names and faces is easy, and best of all—*fun!*

The Six Easy Steps

The most important factor in remembering names and faces is to be interested in people. Set forth a positive attitude, and keep this attitude in the uppermost part of your mind at all times.

Say, "yes! I'm going to remember that name!" You will find it is easier from the beginning. Now for the six secret ingredients in the formula for names and faces.

1. Attention! Get the Name

Most introductions are given in a hasty manner . . . names are slurred or mumbled, and the average person will say, "How do you do," many times not knowing whom he has met!

You can't remember a person's name unless you hear it clearly. When introduced to someone for the first time, *you* control the situation. DON'T BE RUSHED! Make certain you have heard the name correctly. If not, ask the person to repeat it for you. If you still don't hear it clearly, ask the person to spell it. By this time the idea will have gotten across: you want that name!

2. Repeat the Name

Repeat the name immediately. Say, "How do you do, *Mr. Jones*," not

just "How do you do?" This is also an opportunity to check whether you heard the name correctly.

Most people say, "I remember the face, but not the name." This is true because as they look at the person, they get thousands of visual impressions of the person's face, but usually only hear the name a few times. Auditory impressions of the name are important because it is the beginning of the association of the name with the face.

3. Observe the Face

Every face has some outstanding feature or characteristic that distinguishes it from any other face. No two are exactly alike, even in "identical" twins. Just be observant and you will see the difference.

The introduction affords an excellent opportunity for you to observe the face. *Do not be obvious:* it is not necessary to remark, "Would you please turn your head, so I can look at your ears?!" Be aware that you are observing and your eyes will automatically notice these outstanding features.

It is not wise to rely solely upon such things as clothing, for they may change before you see the person again. The one thing that will not change is the individual's features. Study the Chart of Outstanding Features and use it. It will prove helpful in choosing the outstanding facial features that distinguish one person from another.

HOW TO REMEMBER NAMES AND FACES 99

Every Face Is Different

Every person has at least one feature or characteristic that distinguishes him from everyone else. You need not be obvious by staring at an individual

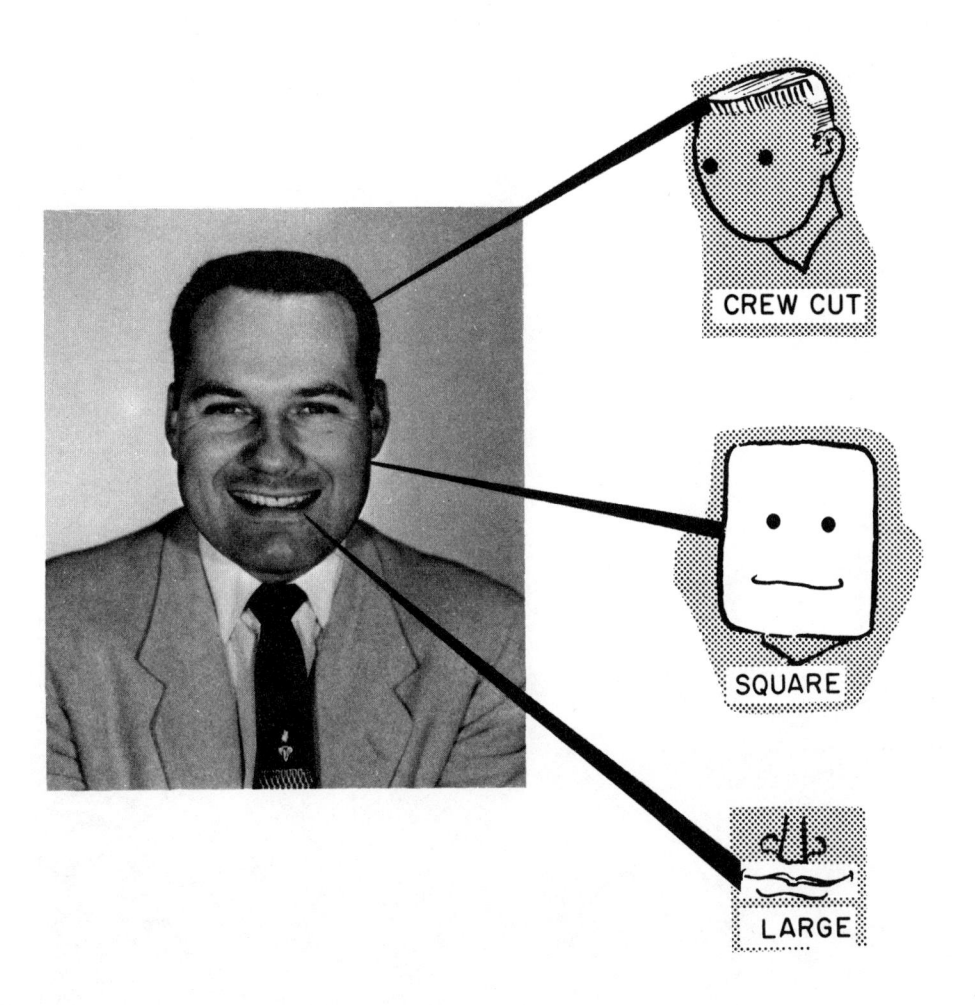

to notice this characteristic. Just observe casually, at the time of introduction for such points as bushy eyebrows, round face, etc.

Study and become familiar with the Chart of Outstanding Features which follows, and you will begin to notice characteristics quickly and easily. An example of the way in which you should choose these characteristics is illustrated with the next photograph. Notice the outstanding characteristics and how well they fit the person. Remember that proficiency comes with use.

CHART OF OUTSTANDING FEATURES

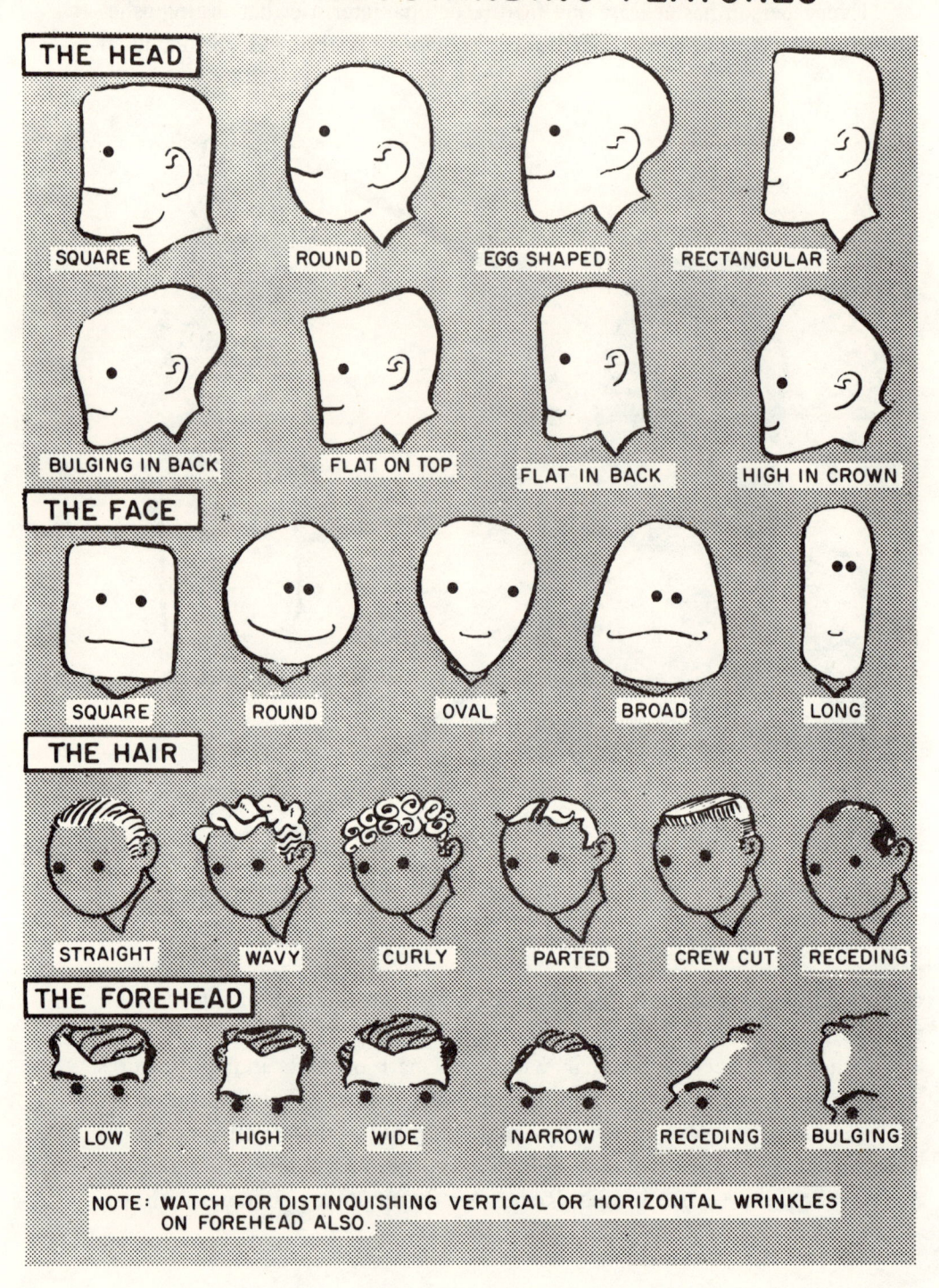

THE HEAD

| SQUARE | ROUND | EGG SHAPED | RECTANGULAR |

| BULGING IN BACK | FLAT ON TOP | FLAT IN BACK | HIGH IN CROWN |

THE FACE

| SQUARE | ROUND | OVAL | BROAD | LONG |

THE HAIR

| STRAIGHT | WAVY | CURLY | PARTED | CREW CUT | RECEDING |

THE FOREHEAD

| LOW | HIGH | WIDE | NARROW | RECEDING | BULGING |

NOTE: WATCH FOR DISTINQUISHING VERTICAL OR HORIZONTAL WRINKLES ON FOREHEAD ALSO.

THE EYEBROWS

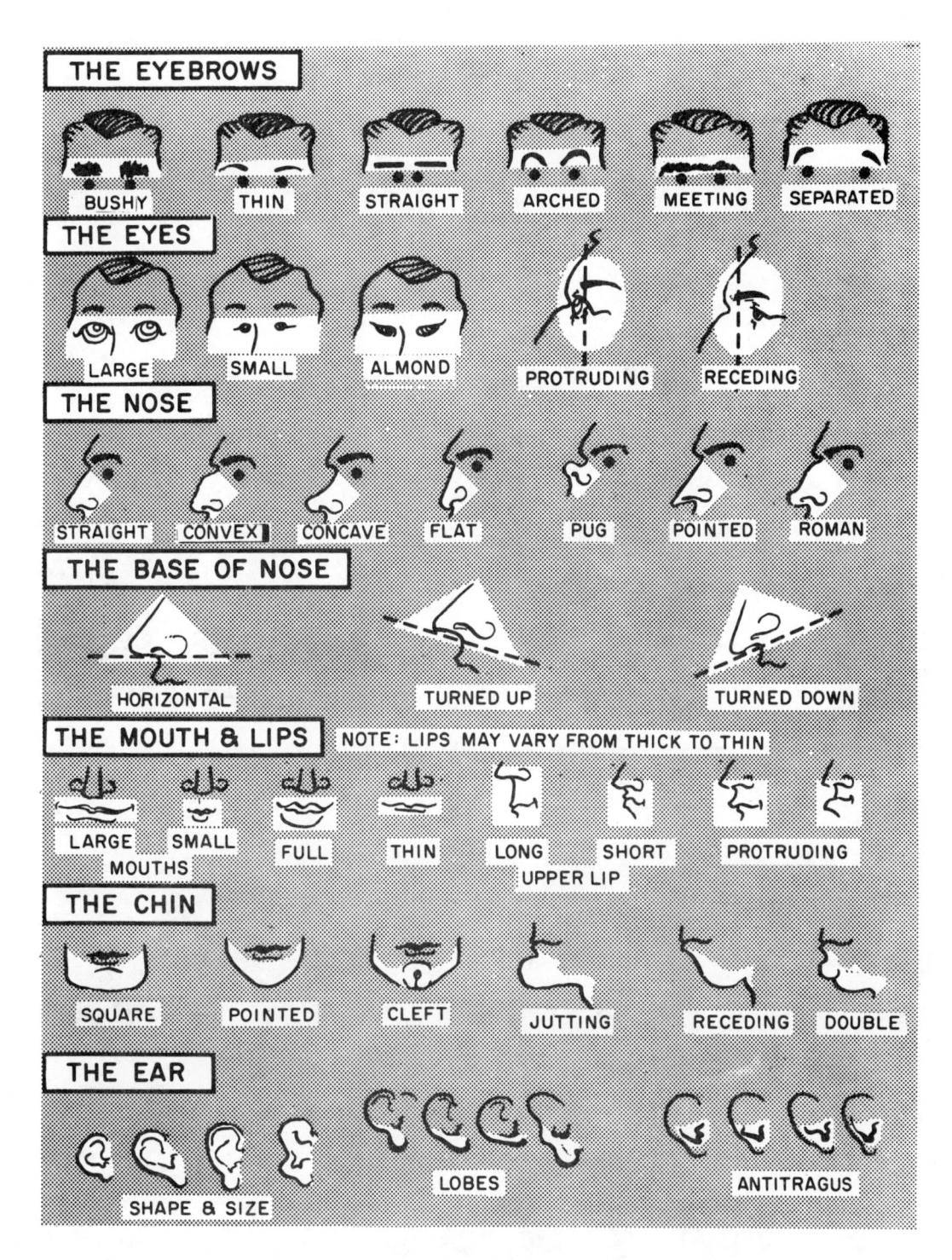

BUSHY · THIN · STRAIGHT · ARCHED · MEETING · SEPARATED

THE EYES

LARGE · SMALL · ALMOND · PROTRUDING · RECEDING

THE NOSE

STRAIGHT · CONVEX · CONCAVE · FLAT · PUG · POINTED · ROMAN

THE BASE OF NOSE

HORIZONTAL · TURNED UP · TURNED DOWN

THE MOUTH & LIPS

NOTE: LIPS MAY VARY FROM THICK TO THIN

LARGE · SMALL MOUTHS · FULL · THIN · LONG · SHORT UPPER LIP · PROTRUDING

THE CHIN

SQUARE · POINTED · CLEFT · JUTTING · RECEDING · DOUBLE

THE EAR

SHAPE & SIZE · LOBES · ANTITRAGUS

102   HOW TO REMEMBER NAMES AND FACES

Find the Features

On these pages are the pictures of 12 different individuals. Use your observation and apply the Chart of Outstanding Features. Find three out-

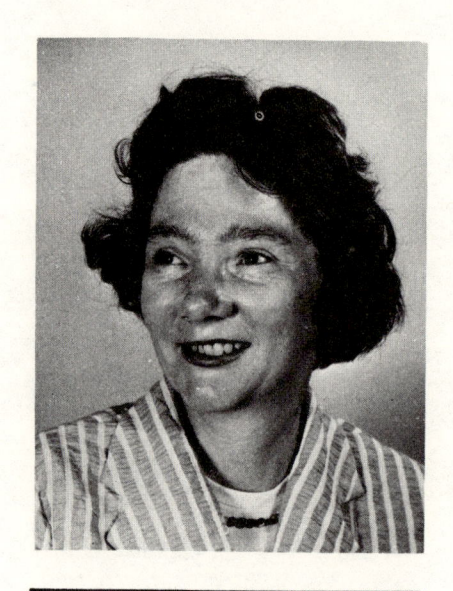

HOW TO REMEMBER NAMES AND FACES 103

standing features on each person. Write these features on the lines underneath each picture. With practice, you will notice that features will be easily and quickly recognized.

FIND THE FEATURES (*cont.*)

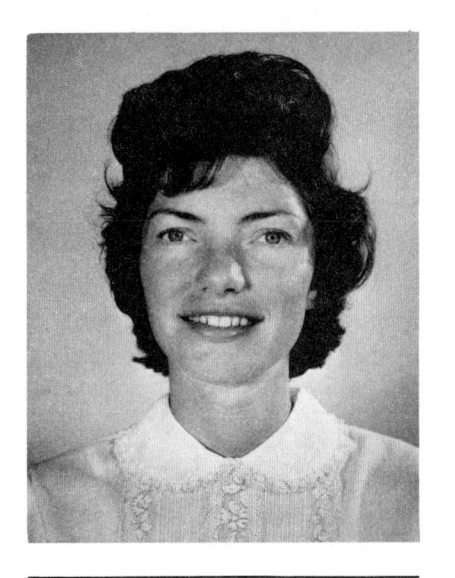

104   HOW TO REMEMBER NAMES AND FACES

4. Associate the Name

To have a person's name at your immediate command, use your ability to associate. One of the most important secrets in remembering names and faces is association.

In the past, you have probably noticed that you had no difficulty with names similar to or identical with some you already knew. Either someone with whom you went to school, a business contact, a friend or relative, an object, names of animals or cities.

What you have been doing, subconsciously, is using association to remember these names. You should now begin associating, *consciously*, names that previously would have held no meaning for you.

When you are introduced to someone for the first time, listen closely to his name and think quickly—what does it sound like? Do I know someone personally with the same name? Or is the name the same as that of a movie star, political figure, product, company, objects? Realize that your mind can go back to thousands of names that you have heard before.

There are various ways in which a name may be associated. Ten ways are listed below. These techniques will benefit you in associating names, just as the Chart of Outstanding Features aided you in quickly observing facial features and characteristics. You may be able to think of categories for names other than the 10 listed here. If so, recognize the category and think of names which belong to it. *Note:* The following chart refers mainly to names listed in point A., Obvious Meaning (category of associations). See page 105.

Ten Techniques for Associating Names	
1. People you already know	Johnson—schoolmate from your home town. Atkins—owns local drug store. Scott—client in business.
2. Political figures	Franklin—Benjamin Franklin Adams—President John Adams Churchill—Winston Churchill
3. Movie stars	Taylor—Robert Taylor, Elizabeth Taylor Lewis—Jerry Lewis, Joe E. Louis O'Brien—Pat O'Brien, Margaret O'Brien

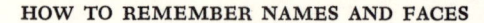

Miss Brady

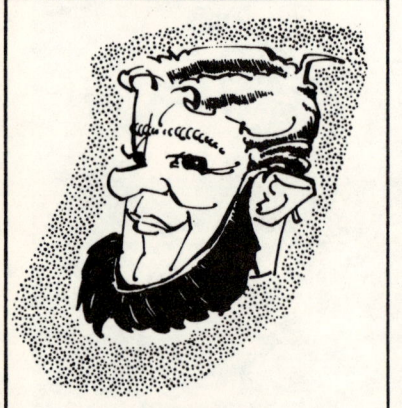

Mr. Beardsley

Miss Hart

Mr. Cameron

4. Occupations	Smith—blacksmith Plummer—plumber Mason—brick mason Baker—baker Shoemaker—shoe maker		
5. Products and companies	Wilson—meats, sports equipment Reynolds—aluminum Johnson—baby powder or wax Stromberg—Stromberg Carlson TV Sears—Sears Roebuck Company		
6. Objects	Glass Stohl Grasser Light	Bell Stone Carr House	
7. Cities or places	London Berlin Washington	Montgomery Houston Austin	
8. Animals	Badger Fox Beaver	Bear Wolf Lyon	
9. Music terms and musicians	Scale Bach Wagner	Harp Dorsey Cantor	
10. Sports terms, sports figures	Ball Ruth	DiMaggio Field	

In association, names may be found under one of two categories. They have been termed:

A. OBVIOUS MEANING—*names such as Bell, London, Baer*
B. NO OBVIOUS MEANING—*substitute by the sound*

Note all the examples given in the Chart of Techniques for Associating Names.

To associate a name without obvious meaning, it is necessary to substitute through similar sounding words. As an example: Dristand sounds like dry sand, or dry stand. Bancroft—bank in a loft. Paparistos—paprika on toast. Pollari—pull hair, or pole air.

Get the idea? Sometimes you'll find that associating the first part of the name will be sufficient to remind you of the entire name, such as bank for *Banc*roft.

Exaggerate your associations and show lots of action. Anything out of the ordinary is much easier to remember.

Now that you have thought of the association, what do you do with it? You can make a picture of the association and see it on the person (working with outstanding facial features and characteristics, whenever possible) or actually see the person doing what your association suggests.

When you see this person again, think before you speak. You want to call him by his name, not *your association*.

Will Rogers, many years ago, told of his experience when he met Mrs. Hummock. He noticed that she was a lady with a protruding stomach. Hummock—stomach. He said he would never forget her name! Then two weeks later while walking down the street he happened to meet the lady again. Thinking back to his association, he blurted out, "Hello, Mrs. Kelly!" (belly—Kelly!)

Think before you speak, and you will call the person by the correct name. Practice on everyone you meet, and with practice, you will become very proficient at making quick and lasting associations.

MASON Mr. Mason has an occupational name, so you can see Mr. Mason as a mason. Picture a Mason jar on his head; he belongs to a Masonic lodge.

HUNTER See Mr. Hunter as a hunter—in the usual hunter's attire. He "brings 'em back alive!"

Use Your Imagination to Associate

As you continue through this chapter, you will find several illustrations of name association. Study each illustration and notice how the name has been made into a picture through the use of the imagination. Apply your own imagination to the names of the people you meet. Say to yourself, "What does the name sound like, does it remind one of a person, place or thing?" Then create your mental picture.

Association of Names

It is important to have speed in making name associations. To gain this speed, practice is needed. The names below are given to you with several suggested associations. These illustrations will give you the idea, then practice on your own with the names and blanks following this list.

NAME	ASSOCIATIONS
Granby	Grand person, plays grand piano, granddad
Post	Wiley Post, Saturday Evening Post, post office
Tracy	Dick Tracy, tracing, Spencer Tracy
Morrow	Edward R. Murrow, burro, borrow, tomorrow

NAME	ASSOCIATIONS
Singer	sewing machine, opera singer
Allison	June Allyson, Alice-in-Wonderland, Allison Engines
Holtz	hold, holster, means wood in German
Fairbanks	Douglas Fairbanks; Fairbanks, Alaska; fair on a bank
Ryder	horseback rider, Red Ryder, writer
Reid	reed instrument, reed, (book) reader
Webster	Webster's Dictionary, Daniel Webster
Bates	Bates Stapler, (fish) bait, Bates bedspread
Preston	Preston Foster, pressed on
Downey	Downey, California; down (as in feathers)
Reynolds	Reynolds Wrap, Marge Reynolds, Debbie Reynolds

Practice Association of Names

Write two or more associations beside each name. Apply the Ten Techniques for Associating Names. Think now! Do you know someone else with the same name—a product, place or any word that the name sounds like?

NAME	ASSOCIATIONS
Campbell	_____
Beale	_____
Devine	_____
Finely	_____
Elliott	_____
Hines	_____
Dempsey	_____
Potter	_____
Powell	_____
Segal	_____
Welch	_____
Steele	_____
Russell	_____
Phillips	_____

JONES When you are introduced to Mr. Jones, beware! The next time you see him, you may recall him as the man with "the easy name." One technique is to see the person's name written on his forehead. This works well at the time of introduction for names that do not bring to mind a quick mental picture. During conversation, develop a stronger association for more lasting retention.

Meet Six People

You have practiced choosing outstanding features by working with 12 people in photographs. You have also practiced thinking of associations for names. Let's apply both techniques to a practical situation. The photographs below are of six of the people you have already chosen features for. Using your imagination and the rules already learned, associate the name with the features on the person's face. Then turn the page and test yourself.

Mr. Appleby

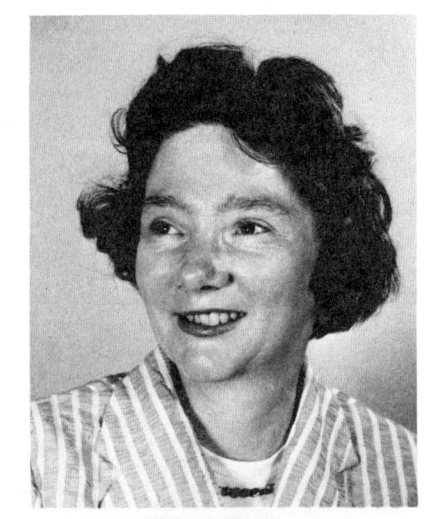

Miss Swanson

Mr. Grey

Mr. Marks

Mr. Flacks

Mrs. Berger

110 HOW TO REMEMBER NAMES AND FACES

Test Yourself

Study the photographs below. Think of your association and then write the name of each individual underneath his picture.

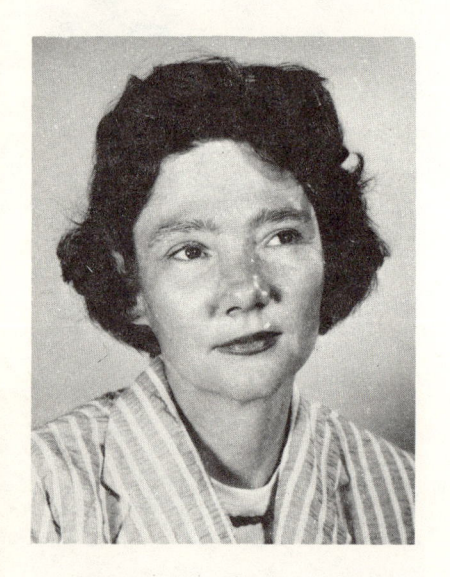

NUMBER CORRECT _____

5. Use Name in Conversation

During the course of conversation with someone, repeat the individual's name several times. You can do this without being obvious by adding it to the end of a sentence. "That's a good example, Mr. Jones." "I have relatives in Ohio, also, Mr. Jones." Do not repeat the name aloud so many times that it becomes annoying to the other person. You can also repeat the name in

your mind without always actually saying it. *Always* calls him by name when saying goodbye, "It was a pleasure meeting you, Mr. Jones."

6. Write the Name Down

Be systematic and record the names of the people you want to remember. Begin now by setting up a system of 3 x 5 cards or a notebook, following the example illustrated. It is most important that the recording take place within 24 hours after you are introduced. Write all the information you can remember, such as:

> Mr. Jones: *red hair, blue eyes, small scar on right cheek, and a square face. Complexion ruddy, stature short and stout.*

List your association for his name, and make sure you picture him again as you write. This is important for lasting retention. The mental and written process involved takes only a few moments. You will find the time well spent and extremely rewarding when you are able to call Mr. Jones by name the next time you see him. An occasional review will insure permanent retention of people you do not see at frequent intervals.

	NAME
	ASSOCIATION
	MET AT DATE
	OCCUPATION, OTHER FACTS
	OUTSTANDING FEATURES
(*Sketch Face*)	

HOW TO REMEMBER NAMES AND FACES   113

Meet Six People

Practice remembering names and faces with the six people on this page. Remember to make good strong associations for the name and tie the name to the outstanding features on the face. Use your power to visualize and see the association *on* the person! Now, I wish to introduce . . .

Miss Farley

Mr. Wheeler

Mrs. Locke

Mr. Partridge

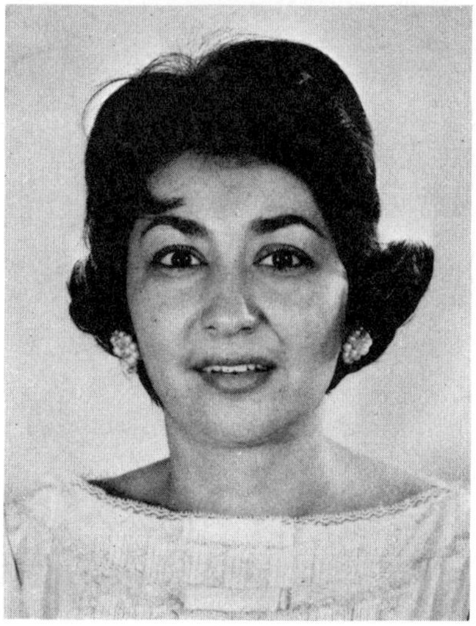

Miss Salazar

Mr. Clark

Test Your Retention

See how well you have improved your memory for names and faces. Look at the person's picture, then think of your association and write the name beneath the picture. Think before you write.

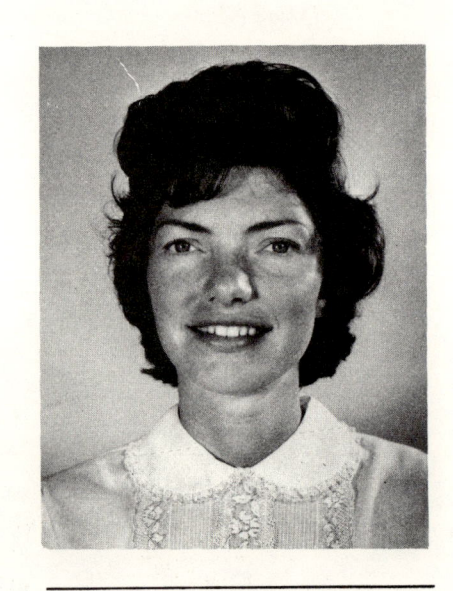

NUMBER CORRECT _____

Additional Practice in Association

By this time you should notice the associations coming to mind faster and with more ease. Write two or more associations beside each of the following names. Use your imagination and make your associations as vivid as possible.

NAME	ASSOCIATIONS
Sharp	_____
Oliver	_____
McBride	_____
Lawler	_____
Curtis	_____
Bender	_____
Josephs	_____
Zeller	_____
McIntosh	_____
Pierce	_____
Hanley	_____
Morgan	_____
Draft	_____
Seward	_____
Schiff	_____
Monroe	_____
Hamilton	_____
Graham	_____

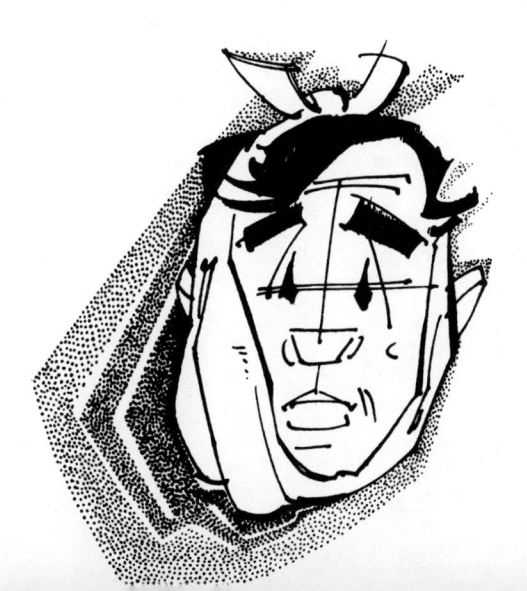

AIKEN Picture him "achin" with a toothache as he waits for the dentist, "aikin'" to get the tooth out. Keep your association pleasant!

For additional practice in name association, have a friend or relative call names and you respond with two or more associations for each name. The Telephone Company has graciously given us thousands of names to practice with. Just consult your telephone directory and skip around, picking names at random. You will never run out of names.

For excellent practice in associating names with individual faces, write names on 3 x 5 index cards, 10 on a card, and take them with you. Go to a place that has people: a cafeteria, park, a bus ride, or in a waiting room — and practice. Example: Sit in a cafeteria and look around the room, mentally assigning a name to each individual. Observe the faces, noticing outstanding features and characteristics. Work in this manner with 10 names at a time, then go back and without referring to the card, call each person by his or her assigned name. If you are with a friend, have him check your accuracy as you go along. If alone, call all ten by name mentally and then check your card to test your retention.

Another excellent practice exercise is to cut photographs from weekly news magazines, take the actual name and associate it with the person's face. You can paste the photos on cards and write the names on the back. Test by looking at the photograph and recalling the name. Or look at the name, visualize the person's face and describe him by recalling his outstanding facial features and characteristics.

This is the ideal way to practice, and you will find that speed comes with practice.

REMEMBER FIRST NAMES AND FACTS ABOUT PEOPLE

Chapter **Eight**

One of the most important facts to remember about people is their first names. You have no doubt observed that you remember the first name of persons you have just met with little or no difficulty. There are three reasons for this:

1. You are more familiar with first names for there are a great number of individuals that you already know with the same first name.
2. There are only 100 male and 100 female first names that are most frequently used.

3. In social groups as well as in business, people are called by their first names more frequently than by their last. This gives you several auditory impressions of the name.

How many people do you know of with the first name "George"? George Washington, King George, George Gobel, just to mention a few.

Write the names of three people that you know personally, or know of, such as historical characters, politicians, movie stars, etc., who have the same first name as:

ARTHUR	HENRY	ROBERT	CATHERINE	MARY	JOAN
_____	_____	_____	_____	____	____
_____	_____	_____	_____	____	____
_____	_____	_____	_____	____	____

You can think of many more first names that are associated with products, movie stars, friends, relatives, streets, cities, political personalities, historical figures.

These names are familiar to everyone. As soon as you hear one of them, think of several people you already know who have the same first name. You can associate the first name with a person by quickly picturing another person with the same name. Then notice how the first and last names can be blended together through sounds:

Marie Ellis . . . Alan Engle . . . Robert Parker . . . George Barnett.

Notice the rhythm or flow of the two names when said together. Say aloud the following names, noticing the rhythmic flow:

Harold Bohannon . . . Glenn Giovani . . . Rebecca Rasmussen . . . Eloise Banks.

Many times you will find that the initials of first, middle and last names will be the same as another person you know:

Fred Donald Reagan (F.D.R.–Franklin *D.* Roosevelt)

Notice alphabetical progressions: *Alice Baker*

Sometimes they form a word or name: *Lola O. Gibbs* (LOG)

John A. Moore (JAM)–*Carol A. Taylor* (CAT)

Also notice the repetition of the same letter at the beginning of the first and last names: *Rebecca Rasmussen, Mary Martin.*

Only the correct name will feel comfortable when you say it, so you would not recall Rebecca as Roberta. If you do not immediately recall the name "Rebecca" you can scan through the alphabet; when you come to "R," it will act as a cue for remembering "Rebecca."

Continue to project your association for the last name onto the individual. The next occasion you have to contact the individual, you will have a point of reference for both first and last names. If you know only his first name, it will be impossible to locate him in the telephone directory. It may be just as difficult to locate him at work, for there may be 10 or more men in the company with the same first name.

Note: Some first and last names tie together very logically, such as: Merry Chase, Seymour Fields, Tom Katz, Penny Nichols, Bea Weiss, Tom Collins.

The following is a list of 100 most popular male and female first names. As you read these names, think of two or more people you know with that particular first name.

One Hundred Popular First Names—Male

John	Paul	Donald	Alan
William	Fred	Lawrence	Chester
Charles	Edwin	Earl	Leo
James	Andrew	Horace	Guy
George	Alfred	Martin	Kenneth
Robert	Peter	Jesse	Otto
Thomas	Ralph	Oliver	Josiah
Henry	Philip	Oscar	Bernard
Joseph	Herbert	Augustus	Claude
Edward	Stephen	Edgar	Christopher
Samuel	Jacob	Anthony	Sidney
Frank	Carl	Patrick	Harvey
Richard	Theodore	Jonathan	Moses
Harry	Clarence	Elmer	Timothy
Francis	Ernest	Stanley	Maurice
Frederick	Michael	Herman	Gilbert
Walter	Lewis	Franklin	Archibald
David	Eugene	Abraham	Jeremiah
Arthur	Hugh	Leonard	Rufus
Albert	Howard	Nathan	Leon

One Hundred Popular First Names—Male (cont'd)

Benjamin	Isaac	Norman	Joshua
Alexander	Nathaniel	Russell	Max
Daniel	Roy	Matthew	Lloyd
Louis	Raymond	Julius	Warren
Harold	Edmund	Nicholas	Roger

One Hundred Popular First Names—Female

Mary	Lorraine	Deborah	Violet
Elizabeth	Irene	Elaine	Beatrice
Barbara	Grace	Carol	Geraldine
Dorothy	Marjorie	Clara	Hazel
Helen	Anna	Edith	Beverly
Margaret	Josephine	Sarah	Norma
Ruth	Louise	Gertrude	Emma
Virginia	Mildred	Sylvia	Gladys
Jean	Janet	Gloria	Adeline
Frances	Evelyn	Rosemary	Stella
Nancy	Marion	Sally	Carolyn
Patricia	Katherine	Edna	Agnes
Jane	Doris	Pauline	Catherine
Alice	Lucille	Julia	Elsie
Joan	Ellen	Joyce	Laura
Betty	Lois	Susan	Constance
Dolores	Marilyn	Jacqueline	Eileen
Eleanor	Martha	Esther	Genevieve
Anne	Harriet	Marian	Rosalie
Florence	June	Theresa	Emily
Ann	Bernice	Kathryn	Cecelia
Rose	Jeanne	Caroline	Joanne
Lillian	Charlotte	Rita	Carmella
Marie	Phyllis	Judith	Vivian
Shirley	Loretta	Priscilla	Lucy

REMEMBER FIRST NAMES AND FACTS ABOUT PEOPLE 121

Meet Six People

You have had an opportunity to practice associations of first names and last names. Now, let's apply what we have learned to an actual situation. You will meet six people again, this time try to remember both the first and the last names. Associate the last name with the individual's outstanding facial features and characteristics, then associate and blend the first name with the last. I would like to introduce . . .

Mr. Virgil Snow    Miss Susan Siegal    Mr. Frank Richter

Miss Jean Carson   Mr. Jim Fairbanks    Mr. Bob Harris

122 REMEMBER FIRST NAMES AND FACTS ABOUT PEOPLE

Test Yourself

How many first and last names can you remember? Test your retention of first and last names of the six people you met on the preceding page.

Your Score _____

Remember Facts About People

It is important for you to remember facts about the people you meet. The business and professional man gains his client's confidence by remembering and mentioning, at an opportune moment, facts that were told to him in a previous conversation. Being able to talk to a person about his business, to inquire about his family, may be instrumental in obtaining a business deal, impressing the boss, or even making new friends.

As an example, the insurance salesman who sees an acquaintance in a restaurant and says, "Harry Smith! Haven't seen you in over a year. Last time I saw you, you were under the weather after having been home from work with a serious case of the flu." Later in the conversation, he takes advantage of an opportunity to remark, "Harry, have you ever thought of Disability Insurance? You know that bout with the flu could have been something worse. You could have been home ill two months, six months or even a year." Harry Smith expressed interest, saying, "How about lunch next Friday so we can talk about it?" At that luncheon Harry Smith bought the Disability Insurance.

If the insurance salesman had not *remembered* this fact and mentioned it at the right time, the policy would not have been sold.

To be a good conversationalist, you should remember facts that have been told to you. What are the facts that we should listen for and remember? A person's occupation, hobby, the car he drives, his marital status, where he was born, his likes and dislikes, general interests, etc. All these facts are important to remember. By knowing them, you will have a point of association, for you probably know someone who has the same occupation, hobby, or who lives in the same general area.

Imagine the embarrassment of an individual who asks a new acquaintance about the health of his five children, to be reminded that he has only two!

Our first step in remembering facts about people is to pay attention and apply good listening habits. Concentrate on what is being said. Visualize these facts and project associations "onto" the individual as he gives them. His occupation or hobby can be seen "on" him. You can picture him actually doing these things.

For example, you meet an individual whose name is Mr. Hull, owner of a lumber company. You can *see* him "hulling" (hauling) lumber for the *hull* of a ship. His hobby is skiing, so picture him "hulling" lumber while skiing. He is also a "hull" of a nice fellow!

Mr. Stone is a plumber. See the individual pounding on a *stone* with a wrench ordinarily used by plumbers.

Practice with the photographs beginning on this page. Tie the name, fact and appearance to the person. Accept these occupations and facts as fitting the person's physical appearance. If it doesn't seem logical, use your imagination! Keep your associations pleasant.

Meet Six People

Turn to page 126 and test your retention of names, faces and facts about people.

Terry Strickland
Writer

Gertrude Thomas
Telephone Company Supervisor

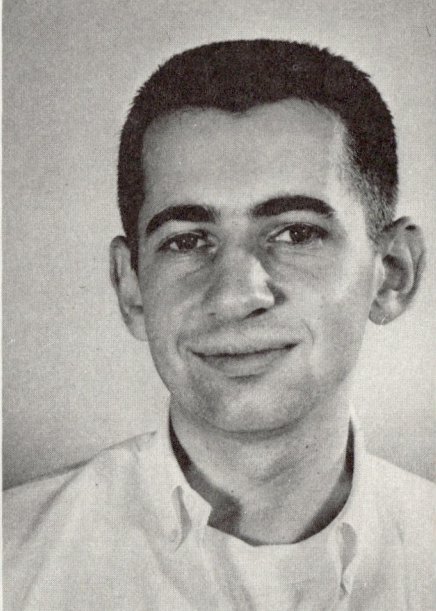

Carl Grushkin
Medical Student

REMEMBER FIRST NAMES AND FACTS ABOUT PEOPLE   125

Leslie Halbert
Building Inspector

Wayne Carter
Pilot

Rosalie Castellano
Owner, Gift Shop

126 REMEMBER FIRST NAMES AND FACTS ABOUT PEOPLE

Test Yourself

Beneath each picture, write the first and last name, and occupation of the individual pictured.

Your Score _____

REMEMBER FIRST NAMES AND FACTS ABOUT PEOPLE   *127*

You can see how easy it is to associate the first and last name, as well as the occupation, with the people you meet. Let's see how we can add more facts and still remember them. The illustration which follows will give you a concrete picture of the way in which this can be done.

Use Your Imagination: Project Your Associations

Mr. Robert Mooney is a retired sea captain. He has seven grandchildren, likes to fish and owns a Great Dane. Notice how all these facts can be pictured and associated with Mr. Mooney in the illustration.

USE YOUR IMAGINATION

PROJECT YOUR ASSOCIATION

Meet Six People

The following six photographs are of ordinary people. Below each photograph is listed information about the individual pictured. The occupation, family information, hobbies, as well as the first and last names, are given. Associate all the facts with each individual and then turn to the next page and test your retention.

Harry Rose
Barber. Likes to go camping. Hobbies: photography and music.

Robert Mooney
Retired sea captain. Has seven grandchildren. Likes to fish. Owns a Great Dane.

Lorraine Hart
Wife of a dentist. Has four children. Likes swimming and painting.

Dusty Mahon
Owner of a travel agency. Hobbies: sports cars and motion pictures.

Eleanor Schager
Real estate agent. Likes golf, boating and gardening.

Glenn Veach
Plumbing contractor. Hobbies: hunting, fishing and stamps.

130.   REMEMBER FIRST NAMES AND FACTS ABOUT PEOPLE

Test Yourself

The people you have just met are pictured again below. Beneath each picture, write the first and last name, the occupation and hobby or other fact that you remember about that individual.

Your Score _____

How to Meet Large Groups of People

In a social or business situation where you will be meeting a large number of people, try to arrive early so you will have time to meet the guests individually or in small groups. Then you can control the situation.

Should you arrive late, you will find the host introducing you to the entire group in rapid succession. Don't be rushed! Stop and get each name clearly and repeat it. Observe the features and make your association. Then, move on to the next individual and repeat the same procedure.

Should you miss a name, it is quite proper to ask the person or the host to repeat it for you. During the course of conversation repeat the person's name. When you see someone sitting alone, practice by trying to recall the name to yourself. Or go over and start a conversation by saying, "How are you enjoying the party, Mr. Jones?" Exchange facts and ideas with this new acquaintance. You will usually find that you have something in common. In a social or business situation, apply the techniques you have learned. You will be more relaxed and have a good time. Remember: Always call the person by name when you say goodbye.

132 REMEMBER FIRST NAMES AND FACTS ABOUT PEOPLE

Final Review

Pictured on these pages are the individuals you have met in these chapters dealing with names and faces. One at a time, study the individual face and

1.  _____ 2.  _____ 3. _____

7.  _____ 8.  _____ 9. _____

REMEMBER FIRST NAMES AND FACTS ABOUT PEOPLE   133

then write his or her name underneath the picture. Score yourself and see how well you have developed your memory for names and faces!

Final Review (cont.)

4. _____

5. _____

6. _____

10. _____

11. _____

12. _____

Final Review (cont.)

13.  _____ 14.  _____ 15. _____

19.  _____ 20. 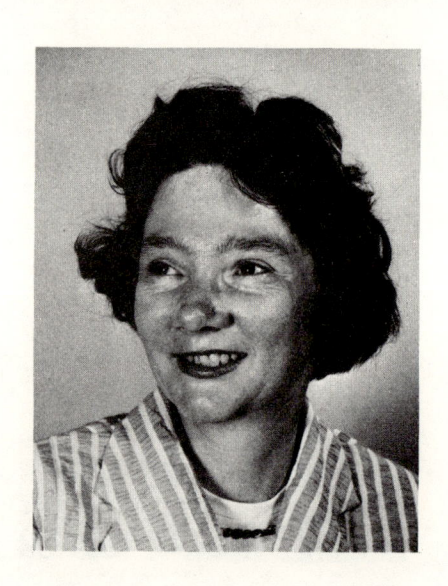 _____ 21. _____

Final Review (cont.)

16. _____ 17. _____ 18. _____

22. _____ 23. _____ 24. _____

Final Review (cont.)

25.  _____ 26.  _____ 27. _____

28.  _____ 29.  _____ 30. _____

Final Review: Answers

Compare the names you assigned to the individuals in the Final Review with the list of correct names below. Then record your final score.

1. Mr. Marks
2. Mrs. Locke
3. Virgil Snow
4. Terry Strickland
5. Lorraine Hart
6. Mr. Appleby
7. Mr. Wheeler
8. Susan Siegal
9. Carl Grushkin
10. Dusty Mahon
11. Mr. Flacks
12. Miss Salazar
13. Frank Richter
14. Gertrude Thomas
15. Harry Rose
16. Mr. Grey
17. Mr. "X" (Never met before!)
18. Mr. Partridge
19. Jean Carson
20. Glenn Veach
21. Miss Swanson
22. Mr. Clark
23. Jim Fairbanks
24. Rosalie Castellano
25. Robert Mooney
26. Mrs. Berger
27. Miss Farley
28. Bob Harris
29. Leslie Halbert
30. Eleanor Schager

YOUR SCORE _____

Review Steps to Remembering Names and Faces

1. Pay Attention and Get the Name.
2. Repeat the Name.
3. Observe the Face: Outstanding Features and Characteristics.
4. Associate the Name.
5. Use Name in Conversation.
6. Write the Name Down.

Be consistent and write the name within 24 hours after you have met the person. When you write the name down, visualize that person's face and especially see his outstanding features and characteristics. Record these features and where you met him, occupation and other important facts about him. Make a rough sketch of his outstanding features. You need not be an artist to do this.

For permanent retention, review your record of names from time to time. As soon as you come to a name, visualize the person's face once again. This review may not be necessary for the people that you see frequently, for every time you see that person, you are reviewing his name and face.

It is suggested that you keep a 3 x 5 card file box with blank cards on your desk. As soon as possible after you meet an individual (do not be obvious by doing this in front of him), take out a card and record all the information as described previously. Arrange these cards alphabetically. In this manner, you will have a constant ready-reference to the person and his name whenever you need it—right at your fingertips!

Remember to apply all the principles given to you in these chapters. You will find your reward not only in dollars and cents profit, but you will suddenly find that people are more interested in remembering *you!*

CONCENTRATE, OBSERVE AND CLASSIFY

Chapter **Nine**

I. It Pays to Observe

We constantly use the power of observation to identify, recall, describe and create.

The importance of observation cannot be overemphasized. Faulty observing has cost many business organizations hundreds of thousands of dollars. Can you term it a mistake when the wrong button was pressed for lack of conscious observation? Not noticing a window left open can lead to robbery—a car tire worn smooth can lead to an accident. The results of wrong medication being administered are obvious.

Mistakes are caused by the lack of conscious awareness. Incidents of everyday life hinge to a large extent on one's observation. Witnesses to an accident or crime often, through incorrect observation, give false testimony unknowingly.

In the task of purchasing a given product, such as a used automobile, one person may notice a detail where another would not. In an auto engine, the presence of a small weld would indicate to the observer that the car had a possible cracked block. The condition of the interior, the cover-up of a flaw in a piece of merchandise, can only be uncovered through one's observation.

One of my students applied his powers of observation in this way. A few years ago, he purchased a deluxe office refrigerator. The cost was $287. The next Monday morning, the delivery men arrived and unpacked the unit from its expensively packaged carton. The new owner was very pleased with the over-all appearance and proceeded to ask questions on its operation and maintenance. Still looking with pleasure over his shiny new purchase he noticed the remains of a white chalk-like compound on the back of the unit. He looked further. Opening the freezer compartment, his eye caught something that would ordinarily go unnoticed by the average person. There was the faint imprint of circles which could have been caused by cans of concentrated fruit juice. At the base, he noticed that the paint was slightly scratched.

His questions changed. Is this a new unit? Why is the paint scratched? Why these circles in the freezer compartment? What is the white compound on the back of the unit?

The driver looked surprised. The purchaser asked the driver to wait one moment while he phoned the company. He spoke with the head of the appliance department and related his findings. The department head acted surprised and said, "Let me check further and I'll call you back in a few moments." Later the phone rang and apologies followed; a mistake had been made. The unit was six months old and had been out on rental, but was still in new condition. The department manager said that if he would keep the unit, they would allow him a $100 reduction in the price. My observant student thought this was fair, and accepted. A little observation and $100 was saved. It pays to observe!

A lady I know parked her car, got out, put a coin in the parking meter for 30 minutes of parking time. Twenty minutes later she came back to her automobile and noticed a parking ticket on the windshield. She was certain that she placed a nickel in the meter. Then she looked around and realized she had placed the nickel in the meter behind her car!

The ability to observe is one of your most important mental tools. What you consciously observe, you will file in your memory. However, you cannot remember a scene or event unless you first see it clearly and register this clear impression in mind. Conscious observation will record firmly in one's mind, over-all details plus supporting details as well as the minutest details.

Two men may look at the same picture. One will say, "That is a beautiful picture," while the other man may enthuse, "Notice that sparkling stream. How I would like to stretch out under that old oak tree with a fishing line! Look at that sunset coloring on those clouds and the strange rock formations." Both of these men looked at the same scene. Only one really saw and projected himself into it. For his conscientious effort in observing, he was rewarded with a richer, more satisfying impression. An individual's enjoyment and reward in life are based upon what he consciously observes.

If you want to remember a person's name and face you must be observant at the time of introduction. A carpenter or engineer must observe every construction detail. A practicing teacher spends one semester as an "observer" in a regular classroom.

A skillful observer will record his impressions exactly as he sees them. If he were an artist he could draw a duplicate scene or if he were gifted with a versatile flow of words, he could vividly describe the form, color or action in the minutest detail.

Your eyes see everything. However, you must consciously *observe* it to recall what your eye has seen. Most people don't remember details because they have not really *seen* them in the first place. The extra second it takes to observe closely and form a mental picture will save time when you need to remember later.

Begin now to sharpen your powers of observation. You will see more, recall more and learn more.

One of my students pointed out her husband's faulty observation. He ran out of gas on Wilshire Blvd. in Los Angeles and had to walk one mile to the nearest gas station. He picked up a can of gas and headed back toward his car. Arriving at the car, he took off the gas cap, poured the gas into the tank, put the cap back on the spout, then placed the empty gas can in the rear of the car.

Sitting in the front seat, he was trying every key in his key ring, but none would fit. It finally dawned on him that the seat covers in his car were grey with silver stripes . . . these were solid blue! The year was the same. This car was the same color but it was someone else's car! Frustrated and disgusted, he proceeded back to the gas station for another can of gas.

This unnecessary frustration and waste of time was caused simply by the individual's lack of observation as to the details of his own automobile and its exact location.

You can increase your powers of observation. The first thing to keep in mind is that you must look to *see*. Practice on the following exercises.

Observation Exercise No. 1

At this moment, could you describe in detail the two houses to the right of yours and the two houses to the left of yours? As soon as possible, look carefully at these houses. Reconstruct them mentally, then describe them to a friend or member of your family. Give all the details you can recall. If you are vague in your description, check again the next time you go past them.

Observation Exercise No. 2

At the dinner table with the family, relax and play this game.

Have everyone observe everything on the table including food, silver, dishes, napkins and tablecloth. Spend two minutes consciously observing. Then everyone should close his eyes and take turns describing what he observed. As each person takes his turn, he should attempt to add what details he can to what has been said before.

Then open your eyes and check to see how accurately you observed.

Observation Exercise No. 3

The area of your own home should be very familiar to you. Test your observation by picturing each room in your home. As you do, try to recall every detail by mentally looking from one part of the room to the other. Then picture your garage and backyard. Check your observation. Make a game out of observing and challenge other members of your family to do better than you. Notice how much more observant everyone becomes.

Practice on the spot! The following is a list of places with which you should be familiar. Practice your observation by describing each place in as complete detail as you possibly can. Then, when you actually visit these places again, check your accuracy.

Dentist's office
Doctor's office
Dashboard of your car
Food market
Dry cleaners
Restaurant (your favorite)
The living room of the home of your best friend
Post Office
Library

Observation Exercise No. 4

Practice your observation of individual faces. You can observe people's faces when you are riding on a bus. Or, when driving and you stop for a red light, look quickly at the driver in the next car. Then look away and try to visualize the driver's face again. Also try to recall all the details of the car—the make, color and body model. All this is done before the light changes. Then look back quickly to check yourself. Don't stare!

This exercise of observing faces will give you excellent practice so that when you apply our rules for remembering names and faces, you will find that your observation practice pays off! It will become automatic and part of your own thinking ability.

Observation Exercise No. 5

Police agencies collect more revenue because of faulty observation than from deliberate traffic violators. This is due to inability to observe signs.

Have you ever received a ticket simply because you didn't observe a posted sign? "No Parking From 7 to 9 A.M. Sunday Excepted," "Loading Zone Only," "One Way Street," "No Left Turn From 4 to 6 P.M.," "Yield Right of Way," "Speed 25 MPH," "Right Lane Must Turn Right," "Temporary No Parking."

Practice sharpening your observation for signs, traffic and otherwise, by consciously observing every sign that you see. Check your Motor Vehicle Code book where all traffic signs are illustrated for you. Associate the shape of each sign with what it means. Then practice on the streets by noticing first the shape of the sign from a distance and recalling what it says before you can actually read it. Notice the location of mail boxes on street corners in front of specific buildings and exact locations.

You would do well to teach the meanings of these signs and their shapes to your family so that they also will be able to recognize signs quickly.

Observation Exercise No. 6

An excellent exercise in developing keen observation is to observe license plate numbers.

While parked behind a car waiting for the light to change, look quickly at the license plate number. Then look away and recall the number. Look back again and check yourself.

Your ability to observe will increase as you practice. Don't stop with these six exercises. There are dozens more that you can create to increase your powers of observation. Sit down and think about it and then practice . . . observe . . . and remember more!

II. Learn How to Concentrate!

Concentration literally means, "to center together." It is an essential ingredient of memorization. You apply thinking techniques of concentration while reading, listening, observing and working on any particular project. If you are genuinely concerned about your inability to concentrate, make improved concentration an immediate objective.

Concentration exercises will develop your ability to control the focusing of the mind on an idea or subject over a prescribed length of time. Learn to exclude everything else from your thoughts. This will eliminate mind-wandering and result in the habit of true concentration. It will help to conserve your energy and produce more efficient work.

Learn to control your attention so that you will be able to cope with any mental task, thereby leading the way to that better memory.

Concentration comes naturally when motive and interest are high. Make your desire to learn stronger than any distraction that might interrupt your progress in learning.

Concentration is often weakened because the individual tenses himself while trying too hard to grasp the idea or mental image.

Do not become tense in order to concentrate. Close the chosen idea in your mind, think about it calmly and mentally visualize it. It takes far less effort to concentrate when you are mentally and physically relaxed. *Remember—concentration and relaxation go hand in hand!* Rid yourself of the basic tensions by relaxing.

The following exercises are designed to help you increase your powers of concentration while sitting in your own home or office. When you complete each exercise, you will notice how little effort was needed to concentrate. You will feel mentally and physically relaxed.

Concentration Exercise No. 1

CONCENTRATE ON ONE OBJECT

Pick up any common object—a watch, a pen, a book, a paper clip, etc., and look at it calmly for five minutes. Observe every detail that you can— its color, size, weight, texture, form, composition, construction, ornamentation. Look at it in whole and in part, without staring, peering or frowning and without any tension whatever. *Remember!* Pure concentration is keeping your mind on a given subject or object, without allowing your mind to wander in another direction. Attention without tension is what is required. Confidence in oneself is also a great help to success in concentration.

Concentration Exercise No. 2

CONTROLLED CONCENTRATION

This exercise is most effective if someone else reads it to you while you concentrate.

Relax and close your eyes. Select a picture of any pleasant scene. For example: Picture a mountain with an airplane flying over the clouds. There is a lake below with two men in a row boat. On the left shore of the lake is a cluster of tall pine trees. On the right shore, see a cow gently grazing. Visualize this scene clearly, then close your eyes and reproduce it in your mind's eye. Mentally look at the entire picture; see it in sharp and clear perspective.

Now begin to eliminate details. First take the clouds out of the picture, now the airplane, the mountain, then the lake and two men in a row boat, then the tall pine trees. Nothing is left in your view but the form of the cow. Eliminate the body of the cow and only see the head and the face. Look at the cow's eyes. Hold your attention for one minute, seeing the cow's eyes clearly. Don't allow your mind to wander for one entire minute.

Now mentally reconstruct the picture. See the cow as a whole again, gently grazing. Bring the tall pines back into the picture, the two men in the row boat, the lake, then the mountains, the airplane and the clouds. Make every effort to see the complete unit with the clearness you were able to see in one small portion. Now, see the entire picture moving off into the distance, getting smaller and smaller, then it stops. Now, bring it closer and closer, see it getting larger and larger, then it stops; then it moves back into the distance until it reaches its original size. Now open your eyes.

Concentration Exercise No. 3

CONTROLLED CONCENTRATION

Try the same exercise using an object, such as a pencil, book or telephone in a familiar room, noticing the surrounding details. Close your eyes and see the room clearly with the object as part. Then slowly make the image clearer and clearer as the other details in the room fade. Then focus your attention on the one object, looking at it from all dimensions. Then slowly bring the entire room back to mind one item at a time, mentally seeing all details as clearly as possible.

Keep in mind that all the methods and exercises in this memory course are designed to increase your powers of concentration. No matter what method you are using to memorize material, you are using your powers of concentration.

You will find that, with practice, your ability to concentrate will increase, and your span of attention and concentration will lengthen.

III. Classification: An Aid to Your Memory

Classification is an orderly arrangement of material into groups, according to related and common characteristics. Everything is subject to classification. As discussed in a previous chapter, the mind has a natural tendency to grasp similarities. This tendency can be used to great advantage.

Often study units are presented in a confused fashion. Writers will sometimes try to cover too much material within a given section. As an example, in learning how to spell, a list of 10 spelling words is given, with one word exemplifying each spelling rule. The mind does not grasp this large amount of abstract material naturally. It would be much better if the author would present each rule by itself, then give five examples illustrating the rule. By the time the student reviews the five spelling words, he could remember the rule. Then move to rule two, rule three and rule four, all using the same type of classified system.

CONCENTRATE, OBSERVE AND CLASSIFY

The same holds true for the study of science, history, mathematics or foreign languages. Likewise, classification is constantly used in school, business, social and home life.

When you classify material in your mind, it is more easily retained. For instance, you can remember a grocery list by classifying the dairy products together, the produce items together, etc. To be efficient, always organize your thinking. Practice grouping items and ideas into their correct categories.

Observe classifications in modern business; food markets, oil companies, or department stores. Efficient organizations have greater profits through less error and wasted time. You can benefit in the same way!

Classification Exercise No. 1

The following items are disorganized. Study them for one minute and notice that they fall into four categories: Kitchen, Sports, Music, Transportation. Close the book and write these 16 items on a separate sheet of paper under the categories in which they belong. Check your score with the items, correctly classified, on the following page.

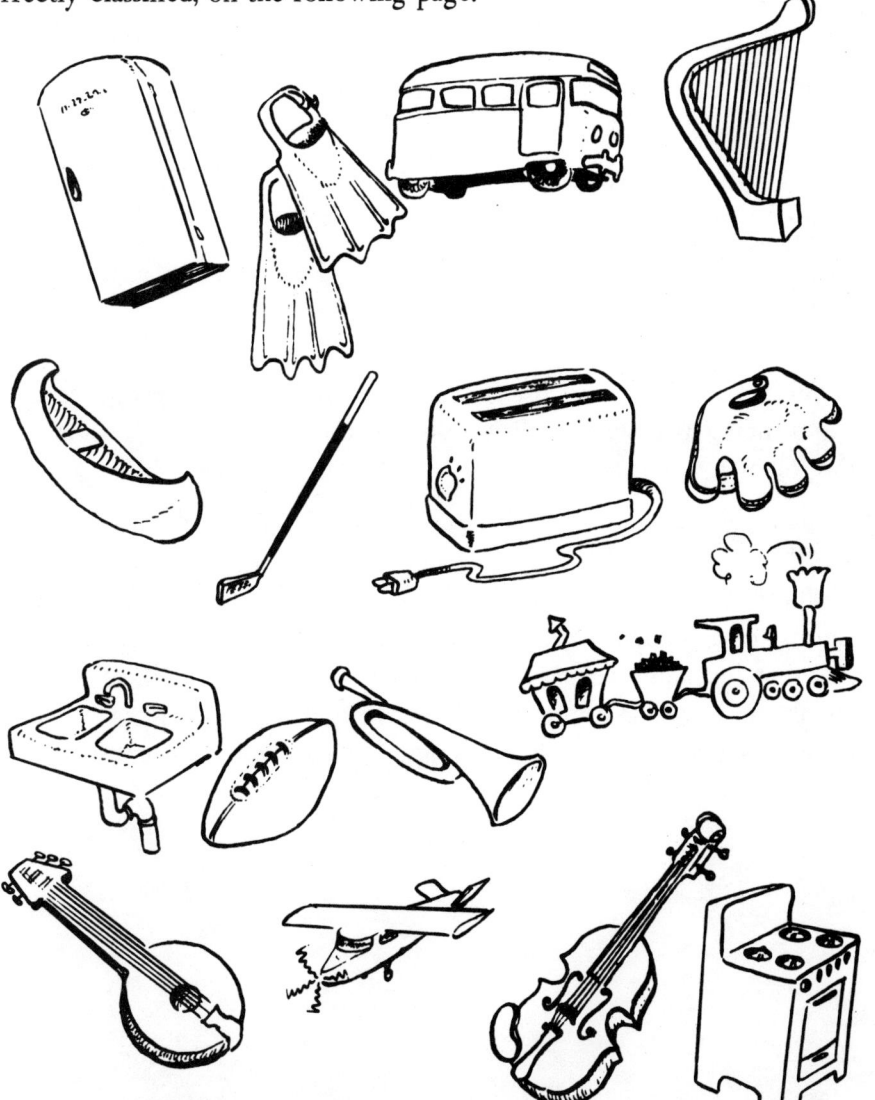

Test Your Classification

The items that you observed and classified on the preceding page are illustrated again below. Notice that they are now classified into their proper categories.

When classifying any list of facts or objects, try to group them together mentally as you study them. Now practice classification on your own in the following exercises.

Classification Exercise No. 2

The following is an unclassified list of 20 words. First read through the entire list, looking for the classifications that they would fit. Then read a second time, mentally placing these items in their proper classifications. Close the book and write the names of the classifications. Then write each item below the classification in which it belongs. Compare your answers to the ones given under the sub-heading, *Test Your Classification*.

CONCENTRATE, OBSERVE AND CLASSIFY   149

Life	summer	Mussolini	Ohio	autumn
Saturday Evening Post	tennis	Danube	Franco	boxing
golf	swimming	Reader's Digest	Hitler	spring
winter	Mississippi	Look	Rhine	Stalin

Test Your Classification

Answers to Classification Exercise No. 2:

MAGAZINES	SEASONS	SPORTS	DICTATORS	RIVERS
Life	summer	boxing	Mussolini	Mississippi
Look	winter	tennis	Stalin	Ohio
Reader's Digest	spring	golf	Franco	Danube
Saturday Evening Post	autumn	swimming	Hitler	Rhine

Classification Exercise No. 3

The following is a list of 16 words which are listed in an unclassified sequence. First, read this list. As you read, mentally organize the classification, noticing which words would fit into the same category. Then close the book. Write the four main categories and list the four words that belong to each classification. Four categories—four words to each category. Visualize as you read these words.

dress	movie	brakes	river
rain	coat	speedometer	concert
hat	ocean	clutch	television
radio	stream	shoes	ignition

Test Your Classification

Answers to Classification Exercise No. 3:

WATER	CLOTHING	ENTERTAINMENT	AUTOMOBILE
rain	dress	concert	ignition
stream	hat	radio	clutch
river	coat	television	brakes
ocean	shoes	movie	speedometer

Classification Exercise No. 4

You have practiced the classification of objects and ideas into the proper categories. Now let's turn the experiment around, to see how well you can name the main classification when you are given the ideas in a classified manner. Practice on these 20 groups of words. Write the main classification on the line under the number of each group. Then check your classifications with the ones on the next page.

1.	2.	3.	4.	5.
___	___	___	___	___
Lincoln	hammer	Verdi	Poe	north
Garfield	wrench	Puccini	Shelley	east
McKinley	pliers	Wagner	Kilmer	south
	saw			west

6.	7.	8.	9.	10.
___	___	___	___	___
orange	Van Gogh	Bach	DeFoe	Ward
pear	El Greco	Brahms	Scott	Sears
apple	Picasso	Chopin	Alcott	Spiegel
lemon				

11.	12.	13.	14.	15.
___	___	___	___	___
see	bass	Salk	La Boheme	Gothic
hear	pike	Curie	Tosca	Ionic
touch	trout	Pasteur	Mme. Butterfly	Doric
taste				
smell				

16.	17.	18.	19.	20.
___	___	___	___	___
Antietam	oil	spaniel	Edison	Asia
Bull Run	water	collie	Whitney	Antarctica
Fredericksburg	lumber	basset	Marconi	Australia

Now compare classifications.

Test Your Classification

Answers to Classification Exercise No. 4:

1. Presidents assassinated
2. Tools
3. Composers of opera
4. Poets
5. Directions
6. Fruit
7. Artists
8. Composers
9. Writers
10. Mail order houses
11. Senses
12. Fish
13. Scientists
14. Puccini operas
15. Architecture
16. Civil War battles
17. Natural resources
18. Dogs
19. Inventors
20. Three continents that begin with "A"

YOUR SCORE _____

Your memory will be greatly aided by learning to classify, in a natural way, the material you wish to learn.

Just as an office runs more smoothly when everything is classified in filing cabinets, so your memory keeps material at ready reference for you when you classify the information you wish to retain. When you want to recall a fact, you just reach into the proper "file drawer" and there it is!

Classification, observation and concentration are all important natural faculties which we possess. It's just a matter now of recognizing the importance of these faculties and using them to the greatest advantage.

HOW TO REMEMBER TELEPHONE NUMBERS

Chapter **Ten**

The average salesperson who calls on clients records their names, addresses and phone numbers in a book which he carries with him. If the salesperson were to lose this precious book, it could be a catastrophe. It could cause untold anxiety, loss of money and possibly even cost a job!

One salesperson I know told me of a nerve-wracking experience he once had. John had an appointment at eight o'clock one evening in Riverside, California, which is 50 miles from Los Angeles. He had written his client's name, address and telephone number in his little book which he always carried in his inside coat pocket.

Right after dinner he got into his car and started the long drive. An hour later, he arrived in Riverside and reached into his pocket for the book. It wasn't there! Frantically, he searched his pockets and then the car, but his efforts were futile. A sinking feeling came over him as he realized that he must have left the book at home on top of his dresser.

He probed his mind for his client's name, or some information that could help him to reach the man he had driven 50 miles to see. He did remember the last name and breathed a sigh of relief as he phoned Information. The response—no such listing. There was no other association in his mind at all! In desperation he telephoned his home so his wife could give the information he needed. The telephone rang and rang, but no answer.

He couldn't keep his appointment, and he didn't make the sale!

Think how simple, how less frustrating it would have been if John had merely spent a few moments memorizing the name, address and telephone number of his client. He wouldn't have needed his crutch, that little address book.

Sales people must constantly prove to their client that they are "on the ball," and the only way to do this is to keep important information in their memory, as well as on paper. If the salesperson is away from the office and needs to telephone a client, valuable time will be wasted looking the number up in the directory or calling Information.

In fact, a statistical survey shows that it requires an average of two minutes to get the number either from Information or from the directory. At peak times during the day, the Information switchboards may be jammed, requiring even four or five minutes to get that number.

If you had to look up five numbers a day, you would waste at least 10 minutes a day. This doesn't sound like much time, but consider the employee or executive who must constantly call Information or consult the directory.

In a five-day period, 50 minutes would be wasted. In one year, it would all add up to 2,600 minutes or 44 hours! More than one complete work week every year wasted just because these telephone numbers aren't memorized.

Most people in business are required to make telephone calls. An average employee earning $200 per week would cost his employer $200 worth of his services every year. Multiply this loss in large corporations and the figure can be astronomical. Notice the chart following:

Time Lost

One Day	One Week	One Year
5 calls	25 calls	1,300 calls
or average 10 minutes	or 50 minutes	or 2,600 minutes
		(approx. 44 hours)

Wages Paid With No Productive Return for Employer

One Employee	100 Employees	1,000 Employees
earning $200 a week	each earning $200 a week	each earning $200 a week
*$200 per year	*$20,000 per year	*$200,000 per year

Imagine the employee who thinks he knows a number, dials it, lo and behold—wrong party. He has to begin all over again: dial Information or look in the directory for the correct number. This time wasted is almost impossible to estimate. "I forgot!" explains, but to an employer it does not excuse—he pays the bill!

Many companies have interoffice communication using the system of telephone extension numbers. I have actually seen employees who have a listing of these extension numbers on a card or in a card file. They constantly refer to this card to dial another department, and time tests show that it takes an average of 31 seconds to find the correct extension number in the card file. The company loses time and money when their employees can't remember these simple, oft repeated numbers.

When you already know a telephone number, or when you have that extension number in your mind, you are more likely to make that call because there is no hassle, so to speak. You don't need to call Information, or look in the directory, or refer to a card. You know the number and feel free to go directly to the telephone and make your call.

There are also times when the Information Operator cannot locate the number you wish as quickly as you need it. Or she may not be able to find it at all because you don't know the correct name spelling. When there is more than one listing for the same name and you don't remember the address, you may have to call three or four numbers to find the person you want. If you must reach your party before a certain time, you may not get through until it is too late. The person you are calling may have already left, making it necessary for you to call again later or the next day.

When calling from a phone booth you must make two calls—first to Information, and then to your party. If the number is unlisted, then you've had it! You can't complete your call until you are back at your office and have your little black book at your disposal again.

Invest time now to remember your telephone numbers and you will find as you save time day after day, week after week, the few moments spent impressing this number into your mind will more than repay itself.

The following techniques give you a means of keeping hundreds of telephone numbers at your fingertips. It is not necessary to call Information constantly for the same number once you have associated it into your mind.

To make telephone numbers easy to remember, you will use our Numerical Alphabet and system called Visual Keys. Using consonants, which have numerical values, and vowels, which have *no* numerical values, we will make words represent numbers. The words which represent numbers will be associated with the person or business firm to whom that number belongs, then when you need the number again, translate these words back into numbers by the Numerical Alphabet.

Here is our Numerical Alphabet, which will be the basis for the words that will represent numbers. Know it well so that you will be able to translate the words back into numbers quickly with ease and confidence.

NUMERICAL ALPHABET

1	2	3	4	5	6	7	8	9	0
t	n	m	R	L	J	K	f	P	z
d					G*	C**	v	B	s
th					dg	G**	ph		c*
					sh	Q			
					ch	ng			
					tch				

* Soft Sound
** Hard Sound
Note: Vowels a, e, i, o, u, and w, h, y, have no number value.

Memorize the Telephone Area Codes

When dialing direct to a telephone number outside your area it is necessary that you dial an Area Code number before dialing the telephone number. Therefore, we will begin by associating the Area Code numbers of major cities in the United States and Canada.

Following is a list of cities and their telephone Area Codes. Memorize this list by associating a word that represents the number, to the city. Use Linking Thoughts and imagination when making your associations. The illustration which follows will give you a vivid impression of the way in which you may make a strong visual picture in your mind of the word that represents the Area Code number, permanently associating it with the city

it represents. When you have memorized all the Area Code numbers given, test your retention.

San Francisco, Calif. Area Code—415

Using the Numerical Alphabet, *R* is 4. *T* is 1, and *L* is 5. Combining the three consonants with vowels, which have no numerical values, the word RaTTLe comes to mind. Translate "rattle" back into a number—415. (The double "T" sounds like only one "T.") Visualize a baby's RATTLE on top of the Golden Gate Bridge in San Francisco.

Continue on your own. The suggested associations given may help you to make a strong visual picture in your mind. Notice how the names of cities which seem abstract have been associated by the *sound* of the name, such as "blocks" for Biloxi, "lost angel" for Los Angeles, etc. If a different association should come to your mind, then use it! Ready? Go!

CITY	AREA CODE NUMBER	WORD	ASSOCIATION
New York City, N.Y.	212	antenna	Antenna on Empire State Building.
Chicago, Illinois	312	mutiny	Mutiny in Chicago.
Los Angeles, Calif.	213	anatomy	See the anatomy of a lost angel.
Miami, Florida	305	measle	People on Miami Beach have one measle.
Washington, D.C.	202	ensign	Our President, in Washington, is putting a medal on an ensign.
Philadelphia, Pa.	215	noodle	See a filly eating noodles.
Salt Lake City, Utah	801	feast	Have a feast on the salt lake.
Las Vegas, Nevada	702	casino	Just another casino in Las Vegas.
St. Louis, Missouri	314	motor	Motor to St. Louis.
Boston, Mass.	617	watchdog	The watchdog was at the Boston Tea Party.
Syracuse, N.Y.	315	medal	He put syrup cues on his medal.

HOW TO REMEMBER TELEPHONE NUMBERS

CITY	AREA CODE NUMBER	WORD	ASSOCIATION
Niagara Falls, N.Y.	716	cottage	Honeymoon in a cottage at Niagara Falls.
Columbus, Ohio	614	chatter	In 1492, Columbus chattered on the ocean blue.
Rochester, Minn.	507	woolsock	Rock chess board stuffed into a woolsock.
Dallas, Texas	214	winter	A doll with lace dressed for winter.
Houston, Texas	713	academy	Visualize a huge stone academy in Texas.
Durango, Colorado	303	museum	He drank V.O. at the museum.
Annapolis, Maryland	301	mast	Mast on the ships at Annapolis.
Abilene, Texas	915	bottle	Abby leans on her bottle.
Rhode Island	401	roost	Rhode Island roost.
Biloxi, Miss.	601	chest	Put blocks in a chest.
Augusta, Maine	207	nice-hick	A gust of wind blew a nice-hick down Main St.
Chattanooga, Tenn.	615	shuttle	Shuttle off on the Chattanooga Choo-Choo.
Raleigh, N.C.	919	bad-boy	Raleigh was a bad-boy.
Montreal, Canada	514	letter	A Mountie always gets his letter.
Vancouver, Canada	604	chaser	A van mover chases her.

When you have associated all these Area Code numbers in your mind, take a test of your retention on the next page.

Test Yourself

The following is a list of the cities with which you have just associated Area Code numbers. Next to the name of the city, write the word which you associated with that city, and then translate that word back into a three-digit number. This number is the Area Code for that particular city. If the picture does not come to mind immediately, continue on with the next one. When you have recalled all the Area Codes that you can, then go back and compare your answers with the original list that you memorized.

CITY	WORD	AREA CODE NUMBER
New York City, N.Y.	_____	_____
Chicago, Illinois	_____	_____
Los Angeles, California	_____	_____
San Francisco, California	_____	_____
Columbus, Ohio	_____	_____
Miami, Florida	_____	_____
Washington, D.C.	_____	_____
Dallas, Texas	_____	_____
Vancouver, Canada	_____	_____
Rochester, Minnesota	_____	_____
Philadelphia, Pa.	_____	_____
Houston, Texas	_____	_____
Salt Lake City, Utah	_____	_____
Durango, Colorado	_____	_____
Syracuse, N.Y.	_____	_____
Las Vegas, Nevada	_____	_____
St. Louis, Missouri	_____	_____
Annapolis, Maryland	_____	_____
Montreal, Canada	_____	_____
Abilene, Texas	_____	_____
Rhode Island	_____	_____
Biloxi, Mississippi	_____	_____
Boston, Mass.	_____	_____
Augusta, Maine	_____	_____

CITY	WORD	AREA CODE NUMBER
Chattanooga, Tennessee	_____	_____
Raleigh, N.C.	_____	_____
Niagara Falls, N.Y.	_____	_____

NUMBER CORRECT _____

Extension Numbers: Apply the Same Technique

Example: Mr. Barlow—extension 942.

To represent Mr. Barlow's name, use the sound of the name—bar-low—and picture a bar that is low. To represent the extension number 942, *BaRN*. Put the two pictures together, and see a *bar* that is *low* all around the *barn*. Logical? When you think of Barlow again, the sound of bar-low will bring back the picture—around the BARN, 942.

Miss Cameron—extension 847. *Camera* for Cameron and *FRoG* for 847. See a FROG sitting on a CAMERA.

Continue to add additional Area Codes and extension numbers to the ones you have memorized. When selecting a word to represent an Area Code, in some instances the most appropriate word to represent the number may have more than three consonants. This would give you more than three digits when translated. However, since you only need three digits, you would translate only the first three consonants and disregard the remaining consonants.

A week from now, test yourself once again on the Area Codes you have memorized. If some of the associations do not come back to mind, then go back over the associations and make a stronger mental picture. The more you practice, the more proficient you will be.

Street Addresses

Apply the same technique to remember street addresses as used in remembering Area Code numbers when the address is a three digit number. If there are four or five digits in the address, then apply the technique which you will learn and apply to complete telephone numbers. Remember: Associate the address with the person or place that it represents.

Watch Repair Shop: 792 Pine Tree Drive

Visualize this shop as a CABIN with a large watch swinging from it, and a huge PINE TREE alongside. *CABIN* for 792—PINE TREE.

Remember Telephone Numbers

When you need to memorize a telephone number, the first thing you should do is to look for logic in the number. A combination of 123-4567 would be obvious and need no special association. Or 246-1492, which would remind you of 2-4-6 and 1492 (Columbus discovered America). 135-1776 has meaning—1-3-5 and 1776 (Declaration of Independence); 987-1066—9-8-7 and 1066 (Battle of Hastings).

Exchanges and Exchange Numbers

If your city uses letter prefixes, then you would make a word from the two prefix letters and the prefix number: HO 9—*HOP*.

The HO in HOP represents the HO in the prefix and the first consonant which follows these two letters represents the prefix number—P for 9. HOP— HO 9.

Examples: Exchanges and Exchange Numbers

The following is a list of exchanges and exchange numbers found in various cities in the United States. The words suggested to represent these exchanges and exchange numbers will illustrate how this information may be memorized and applied to the exchanges and exchange numbers in your own area.

MUtual	PLeasant	WEbster
MU. 3–MUM/PS	PL. 1–PLATE	WE. 1–WET
MU. 4–MUR/AL	PL. 2–PLANE	WE. 2–WEIN/ER
MU. 5–MULE	PL. 3–PLUM	WE. 3–WEIM/araner
MU. 6–MUSH	PL. 8–PLAYF/UL	WE. 4–WEAR
MU. 7–MUG	PL. 9–PLAYBOY	WE. 5–WELL
		WE. 6–WEDGE
		WE. 8–WEAVE
		WE. 9–WEB

CLinton   RIchmond
    CL. 4–CLEAR   RI. 7–RICK/SHAW
    CL. 6–CLUTCH   RI. 8–RIF/LE
    CL. 7–CLOCK   RI. 9–RIB

HOllywood   LOrain   VAndike
    HO. 2–HONEY   LO. 4–LORE   VA. 1–VAT
    HO. 4–HOR/N   LO. 6–LODGE   VA. 2–VAN
    HO. 5–HOLE   LO. 7–LOCK   VA. 9–VAP/OR
    HO. 7–HOG   LO. 9–LOBBY

CRestview   GArfield   HEmlock
    CR. 1–CRAD/LE   GA. 1–GATE   HE. 2–HEN
    CR. 4–CRIER   GA. 2–GAIN   HE. 3–HEM
    CR. 5–CREEL   GA. 3–GAM   HE. 4–HEAR
    CR. 6–CRUTCH   GA. 4–GAR/AGE   HE. 5–HEEL
                       GA. 5–GALLEY   HE. 6–HEDGE
                       GA. 7–GAG   HE. 7–HECK/LE
                       GA. 9–GAB   HE. 8–HEAV/EN
                                          HE. 9–HEAP

POpular   STate
    PO. 1–POT   ST. 4–STAR
    PO. 2–PON/D   ST. 5–STOLE
    PO. 3–POEM   ST. 6–STITCH
    PO. 5–POLE   ST. 9–STOP
    PO. 6–POACH   ST. 0–STACY

To remember a telephone number that has an exchange and exchange number followed by four digits, the last four digits would be associated with one or two words which would represent these numbers. Sometimes they, too, will be logical. The telephone number of the Hollywood *Citizen-News* (newspaper) in Hollywood, California, is HO 9-1234. You could picture HOP to represent HO 9 . . . HOP 1234, HOP 1234. Or you could use words to represent these last four digits, such as TIN-MARE. Picture yourself HOP 1234, HOP 1234 over to the Hollywood *Citizen-News*, or you HOP onto your TIN MARE to get to the Hollywood *Citizen-News*.

Dentist: MU. 5–8614

Suppose your dentist's telephone number is MUtual 5-8614. To remember this number, you can use three words: *MULE–FISH–TIRE*. Picture these three words tied to the dentist . . . the dentist is working in a MULE's mouth with pliers, but instead of pulling a tooth, he pulls out a FISH and places it into a TIRE, which he keeps on the floor in front of him for just this purpose! To remember that TIRE is the last association, imagine the tire small. The small association is always at the end.

If you already know the exchange, then all you need to remember are the five digits. To do this, you can take two words to represent the five digits, and tie them to the person owning the number.

Dry Cleaners: 71942

Suppose the number of Spotless Dry Cleaners was 71942. Tie the words: CAT and BARN to the Cleaners. Picture the Cleaners' building in the form of a BARN which has a huge CAT on top of it. <u>CA*T*</u> and <u>*B*AR*N*</u>–71942.

In this system, the two-digit word is the first association and the three-digit word is the second. Try to be consistent, for this will avoid a possible transposition.

Other examples of words to represent telephone numbers when the prefix is already known:

39584	94857
MOP–LOVER	BAR–FLAG
17962	51743
TAG–PIGEON	LIGHT–CREAM

Whether you find logic in the telephone number to be remembered or make words to represent the numbers, the important thing is the end result: remembering the telephone number when you need it again.

All Number Dialing

Telephone companies throughout the United States today are changing to all numeral dialing. In this system they are replacing the prefixes with the equivalent numbers on the telephone dial.

Now, let's associate all numeral telephone numbers with the person or place that they represent. The telephone numbers in this section are places of interest or government offices. They will give an example of how our methods are applied. Although you may never call one of these numbers, memorize them for the exercise. Then when you need to apply these techniques to your own list of telephone numbers, it will be easier because you will have already developed the skill.

HOW TO REMEMBER TELEPHONE NUMBERS

In most large cities, telephone numbers are made up of seven digits; the first three digits are the prefix numbers which indicate the area of the city in which the telephone is located, and the last four digits pinpoint that particular telephone. The prefix numbers, or the first three digits of the telephone number, will be your first association. Besides this type of grouping of numbers, practice the other techniques for breaking the telephone number into different association groups. Then apply the one that works best for you.

City Hall, Los Angeles: 624–5211

$$\begin{matrix} 6\ 2 & 4\text{--}5 & 2 & 1 & 1 \\ \text{JuNioR} & \text{--LioN--} & \text{TooT} \end{matrix}$$

Picture a little boy, JUNIOR, holding onto his LION who makes the horn go TOOT!

The number of City Hall has been changed to 485-2121. Create a new picture. See a big **rifle** and a **net net**. You can change your old picture to a new picture!

Now that you have the idea, practice on the following telephone numbers. The telephone number is listed with words underneath. These words have been chosen because according to the Numerical Alphabet, they represent the number to be remembered. In the following numbers, a word has been chosen to represent the first three digits, and either one or two words to represent the last four digits. When translating these words back into numbers, translate the word which represents the three-digit number first. Create a strong visual picture of each telephone number tied to the place to which it belongs. Remember to use your imagination!

PLACE	TELEPHONE NUMBER	ASSOCIATION
F.B.I., Los Angeles, Calif.	477-6565 wrecking jail jail	See the F.B.I. wrecking a jail jail
U.S. TREASURY Washington, D.C.	566-2000 ill judge nose sauce	See an ill judge with his nose in sauce
MUSEUM OF NATURAL HISTORY, New York City	873-4225 vacuum ruin Nile	See a vacuum on the ruin on the Nile

F.B.I., Chicago: 431–1333

4 3 1–1 3 3 3
heRMiT–TaM–MuMMy

Picture an FBI man arresting a HERMIT wearing a TAM and carrying a MUMMY. FBI-431-1333.

HOW TO REMEMBER TELEPHONE NUMBERS

You have just applied the technique of dividing a telephone number into parts, memorizing the first three digits first, then the last four. Let's continue to apply this technique with some variations. Another technique is to place an actual number in front of the key word such as 7 LILY for 755. Practice on the following numbers, noticing the suggested words and the associations will stimulate your imagination, helping you to remember these numbers.

PLACE	TELEPHONE NUMBER	ASSOCIATION
FEDERAL INFORMATION CENTER, Washington, D.C.	755-8660 7 Lily, fish cheese	At the Information Booth, see 7 Lily in fish and cheese.
DEPT. OF HEALTH, EDUCATION AND WELFARE, Washington, D.C.	655-4000 6 Lily Rose Sauce	See 6 Lily in a rose sauce.
DEPT. OF INTERNAL REVENUE, New York City	732-0240 kimona sunrise	When you pay taxes, wear a kimona at sunrise
PUBLIC LIBRARY, New York City	790-6161 cabs jet jet	Cabs jet jet.
EMPIRE STATE BLDG., New York City	736-3100 gumshoe mat sauce	See gumshoe mat sauce.
MAYOR, Columbus, Ohio	222-7671 2 nun cash kit	See 2 nuns with a cash kit.
DODGER STADIUM, Los Angeles, California	224-1500 noon hour tail see-saw	At Dodger Stadium, noon hour, a tail is on the see-saw.
MAIN POST OFFICE, Los Angeles, California	688-2290 shove off nun booze	Shove-off nun with booze.
TREASURE ISLAND, San Francisco, California	765-9111 egg shell bed tide	See the eggshell in a bed, floating around Treasure Island.

When using any key word from 11-tide to 99-baby together, make the first association larger and the second association smaller. Example: Treasure Island phone number, See a huge bed — small tide.

PLACE	TELEPHONE NUMBER	ASSOCIATION
LOS ANGELES PUBLIC LIBRARY, Los Angeles, California	626-7461 6 inch-car jet	Picture a 6 inch book on a car jet
LOS ANGELES COUNTY SHERIFF'S DEPARTMENT Los Angeles, California	974-4211 poker rain tide	See the sheriffs playing poker in the rain tide.
WALTER REED HOSPITAL Washington, D.C.	545-6700 laurel jug sauce	See Laurel with a jug and sauce
HOUSTON POST, Houston, Texas	621-7000 giant kiss zoos	See a giant kiss zoos.
SMITHSONIAN INSTITUTION, Washington, D.C.	628-4422 gin-f/izz rare onion	See a gin fizz on a rare onion.
PENTAGON, Washington, D.C.	545-6700 lawyer-logic-aces	Pentagon lawyers are logic aces.
STATE DEPARTMENT, Washington, D.C.	655-4000	NOTE: The State Department is the same as the Department of Health, Education & Welfare.
MAYO CLINIC: Rochester, Minnesota	Area Code 507-282-2511	

The Area Code for Rochester, Minnesota is 507-WOOLSOCK. Three words to represent the telephone number 282-2511: INFANT-NEWLY-TOOTH. Notice the illustration. This is the picture you should have in mind for an Area Code and telephone number tied to the place that it represents. NOTICE: Only translate the first three consonants in the word INFANT to give 282 FNT.

HOW TO REMEMBER TELEPHONE NUMBERS

Test Yourself

Take a test of your retention. Write the Associations, Area Codes and Telephone Numbers that you have just memorized.

PLACE	ASSOCIATION	AREA CODE AND TELEPHONE NUMBER
U.S. Information Service, Washington, D.C.	_____	_____
State Dept., Washington, D.C.	_____	_____
Dept. of Health, Education and Welfare, Washington, D.C.	_____	_____
Dept. of Internal Revenue, New York City	_____	_____
U.S. Treasury, Washington, D.C.	_____	_____
Public Library, New York City	_____	_____
Empire State Building, New York City	_____	_____
Mayor, Columbus, Ohio	_____	_____
Dodger Stadium, Los Angeles	_____	_____
International Airport, Los Angeles	_____	_____
Main Post Office, Los Angeles	_____	_____
Public Library, Los Angeles	_____	_____
City Hall, Los Angeles	_____	_____
FBI, Chicago, Illinois	_____	_____
Treasure Island, San Francisco	_____	_____
FBI, Los Angeles	_____	_____
Yankee Stadium, New York City	_____	_____
Blackfoot Indian Reservation, Durango, Colorado	_____	_____
General Hospital, Philadelphia, Pa.	_____	_____
Walter Reed Hospital, Washington, D.C.	_____	_____
Houston Post, Houston, Texas	_____	_____

PLACE	ASSOCIATION	AREA CODE AND TELEPHONE NUMBER
Museum of Natural History, New York City	_____	_____
Smithsonian Institute, Washington, D.C.	_____	_____
Pentagon, Washington, D.C.	_____	_____

Many hours are wasted when you phone Directory Assistance and the recording says, "We're sorry if the number you need was not listed in the phone book. Please stay on the line and when the operator gives you the number, jot it down for future use. Thank you."

APPLY YOUR MEMORY SYSTEM AND SAVE TIME.

It's All-Number Calling

Telephone Number Record

Keep a systematic record of all important telephone numbers you wish to remember. This record is a valuable check list for ready reference and is also used to review associations of numbers not used frequently. The following form is an example, describing how a telephone number record should be kept. Also use 3 x 5 card system for review away from home or office. Place name and phone number on one side and association on opposite side.

NAME	ADDRESS	AREA CODE	TELEPHONE NUMBER	ASSOCIATION

REVIEW PERIODICALLY TO KEEP NUMBERS FRESH IN MIND.

Sample of 3 x 5 Card Review System

FRONT SIDE | BACK SIDE

NAMES AND PHONE NUMBERS TO REMEMBER

1. _____
2. _____
3. _____
4. _____
5. _____
6. _____
7. _____
8. _____
9. _____
10. _____
11. _____
12. _____

ASSOCIATIONS FOR NAMES AND PHONE NUMBERS

1. _____
2. _____
3. _____
4. _____
5. _____
6. _____
7. _____
8. _____
9. _____
10. _____
11. _____
12. _____

THE CUE METHOD OF MEMORIZING

Chapter **Eleven**

The Logical Cue Method is a system for remembering in which the student selects one or two words from a whole idea to represent that idea. These words are memory joggers called "cues." Think of the cue and the rest of the facts contained in the complete idea will return to mind.

You may or may not be aware of the fact that you have been using a cue system for a long time. For instance, your friend asks you to tell the story about the "drunk." Drunk is the cue word and the whole story comes to mind. Seeing a picture of a chariot reminds you of the movie, "Ben Hur." The number 13 brings to mind the 13 Colonies, Friday the 13th. December 7th reminds us of Pearl Harbor. These, of course, are single cues and bring to mind a specific idea or fact.

In remembering the continuity of subject matter we arrange the cues in a logical order and tie them together by using linking thoughts. Therefore, we have termed them *Logical Cues*. When using the Logical Cue Method, it is important that the correct and most meaningful cues be extracted.

As an example of the cues that can be extracted, we will use the true story of "Lincoln's Failures." Read the following story twice, visualizing as you read. Notice the list of cues below the story that have been extracted. The first three cues are listed with the whole ideas they represent. Reading the other cues, write the whole ideas that were expressed. Read the story again from beginning to end. Each cue should act as a stimulus to bring these whole ideas back to mind. Notice that the cues came from within the story and were the main points that brought the entire idea to mind.

Lincoln's Failures

When Abraham Lincoln was a young man he ran for the legislature in Illinois, and was badly swamped. **He next entered business, failed, and spent 17 years of his life paying the debts of a worthless partner. **He fell in love with a beautiful young woman to whom he became engaged—then she died. **Entering politics he ran for Congress and was badly defeated. He then tried to get an appointment to the United States Land Office, but failed. **He became a candidate for the United States Senate and was badly defeated. **In 1856 he became a candidate for the vice-presidency and was again defeated. **In 1858 he was defeated by Douglas. **But in the face of all this defeat and failure, he eventually achieved the highest success attainable in life.

CUES	WHOLE IDEA
legislature	young man–Illinois–badly swamped
business	failed–17 years–debts of partner
engaged	love–beautiful woman–died, etc.
Congress	
Land	
Senate	
Vice-President	
Douglas	
achieved	
success	
fame	

USE LOGIC. Ask questions (how, what, when, where, why, who). Example: When Abraham Lincoln was a young man, what did he do? ...(ran for the legislature in Illinois.) What happened?...and was badly swamped. What happened next?... he next entered business, failed, etc.

For more permanent retention, memorize the cues that represent this illustration. Link them together to form a sentence. To make a complete thought, use small words between the cues to link them together.

Legislature (had) *business* (and) *engaged Congress* (to) *Land* (the) *Senate* (for) *Vice-President Douglas* (who then) *achieved success* (and) *fame*.

Apply this method of retention to text material, speeches, sales talks, presentations, magazine articles, books, poems, lyrics. Try it on your new insurance policy!

To gain practice in extracting cues from written text, we have chosen two very interesting articles published by the New York Life Insurance Company, and they have given us their kind permission to reprint them.

The first is titled, "Should You Be a Doctor?" At the end of this story, you will find a chart which we have prepared to show how cues may be extracted from this type of material.

First read the story through without stopping to ponder, then go back and read it once again. Go through the chart at the end of the story very carefully, and note your agreement or disagreement with the cue choices. If you disagree with one of the cues, then recognize that your own choice of a cue may be better for you than the one suggested. Keep in mind that the purpose of the cue is to bring the supporting ideas to mind.

Should You Be a Doctor?*

By Walter C. Alvarez, M.D., as told to Morton Sontheimer

The day after I graduated from high school my busy doctor father did something he had never done before—he took me out to lunch with him. After the meal he sat for a minute thoughtfully stroking his goatee. Finally he said, "Well, Walter, what do you want to do as a life work?"

I was surprised. "Why, Dad," I replied. "Am I not to be a doctor?"

He leaned forward eagerly, "You really want to be a doctor?" he asked.

"I have never thought of anything else."

A smile of relief and satisfaction came over his face. I realized at that moment that he would never have urged me to follow in his footsteps. No parent should ever force his child into medicine. Unless a young man or woman truly wants to be a doctor, you cannot expect him to persevere through the long, arduous, exacting years of training.

Many a friend has asked me, "Why didn't you make at least one of your two sons a doctor?" And my answer has been, "I wouldn't attempt to make either of them anything." I've told my children, "You

---
* Copyright by New York Life Insurance Company, 1961. Reprinted by permission.

decide what you want to be and I'll give you the best possible education for it."

The desire to be a doctor, though, is only a first requirement. The other requisites are qualities you will be able to recognize early. If you are considering medicine as your career, ask yourself these questions:

Are your school marks high? You must have a high scholastic record or you will not be accepted by the medical school.

Are you interested in science? I started reading science literature voraciously at the age of 12. I haven't stopped yet. Without scientific interest, I cannot imagine a person being either successful or happy in medicine.

Finally, can your parents give you the financial help you will surely need? This is a sacrifice they must make. It's a considerable one to the average father and mother. Three years in pre-medical college, four years in medical school, two years as an intern and resident, and perhaps three years in a big clinic learning a specialty—12 long years in all—will cost the family some $30,000. Today many deans will not let a man start in medical school unless he has this large sum in sight. Why? Because today the course is so difficult that a student cannot hope to work his way through. After that, let us remember that the young doctor beginning practice may need another $5,000 to fit up his office and to tide him over before he can make a decent living.

Now let's consider some of the subtler qualities, like courage, that a young person should have if he hopes to become a good doctor. For instance, the other night at 10 o'clock I was called to help two able colleagues, a family physician and a surgeon, make a decision.

For ten days a little boy had lain desperately ill. To operate might take away what little chance of life the child had. To let him go the night might mean that by morning he would be too far gone for surgery to help. The terrible decision had to be made and it had to be made right then. We decided to operate.

The family physician called in the young parents. They were understandably reluctant to allow a dangerous operation. Firmly, yet with utmost sympathy, the doctor explained the situation and won their consent. It was hard for me to sleep that night with the outcome of that decision weighing on my heart. And the family doctor—think how hard it would have been for him to face those parents if our judgment had turned out wrong. Fortunately, it didn't. The child got well.

Incidents like that are common in a doctor's life. Often, in some farm house in the dead of night, he has to face them alone and with full responsibility. One such episode tells volumes about the qualities that should be inborn in the physician. Think about these qualities when you contemplate a medical career.

You must not only have good judgment, but the special kind of courage needed to act upon it, when the situation might be fatal. If you are going to be a good doctor, you must have the faculty of leadership and the ability to influence people for their own good. You must be able to remain calm in the presence of danger. You need patience, optimism, equanimity.

For many reasons you should have idealism and honesty, but especially so that people will believe you and believe in you. Above all, you should like people. And it will be well for you to have a strong, robust body because medicine can be the most exacting of jobs. For months at a time it may keep you on call 24 hours out of the 24.

Some of these characteristics may be developed, but the discerning person can look for the beginnings of them in adolescence. The kind of youngster whom dogs and little children instinctively trust gives promise as a future doctor.

The career of medicine is varied enough to accommodate many types of personality. A graduate doctor can become a general practitioner, a specialist, an employee of a large company or of the government, a teacher, a laboratory worker or a researcher. He can work alone or in a big clinic. With his medical degree he can always be reasonably assured of work.

It can bring a good enough financial reward, too. But the wealthy physician so many people have in mind when they think of medicine as a career is like the smaller part of the iceberg that sticks out of water. For every one like him, there are dozens of doctors who just make a comfortable living. The average income of a physician in the United States is about $18,000 a year, according to the latest survey.

More and more girls are going into the profession. I do think, though, that it is easier to discover the young woman who is fitted for it. She will stand out among her sisters even more than does the young man among his fellows. In the first place, it is an unusual young woman who is interested in science. Although women doctors do marry, the girl who will maintain her scientific interest despite considerations of marriage is rare.

Invariably, I believe, this sort of girl will have a strong character, recognizable qualities of leadership and exceptional talents as a student.

Perhaps all this makes the career of medicine seem like a hard and exacting taskmaster. It is, and to state it any other way would be unfair.

But I can say this—there is no finer profession a young person can enter. It offers a high standing in the community and a wonderful opportunity to be helpful to others and to do a great good. I know of no other profession that can give a parent so much pride in the achievements of his son or daughter.

From the moment I set out to be a doctor—and I was so young I do not know exactly when it was—I have never regretted the decision.

Cues to Remember

When extracting cues from this article, "Should You Be a Doctor?" by Dr. Walter Alvarez, you should attempt to extract the least possible number of cues to retain the maximum amount of material.

When you have reduced the cues to a minimum, you should find that eight main cues bring back all the complete thoughts in the article. The following chart shows the main cues, then the sub cues, and finally the thoughts which each main cue represents. Go over these cues and notice how the main cue can serve as a springboard to bring back all the information contained in each thought unit.

Cues Extracted From "Should You Be a Doctor?"

MAIN CUES	SUB CUES	THOUGHTS
Requisites	Desire	First requirement is desire.
	Study Habits	Hardest to learn well.
	Grades	High scholastic record.
	Science	A must to be happy and successful in medicine.
Costs	Schooling	12 years–$30,000.
	Office	$5,000.
Qualities	Courage	Little boy.
	Judgment	Must be able to act upon.
	Leadership	Influence people, remain calm.
	Idealism	Believe you and believe in you; honesty; like people.
Health	Robust body	Exacting job; on call 24 hours.
Types	General practice	Variety assured of work.
	Specialist	
	Industry	
	Government	
	Teacher	
	Laboratory worker	
	Research	
	Clinic	
Financial Reward	Wealthy physician	The exception.
	Average income	$18,000.
Women Doctors	Unusual woman	Marriage; recognizable qualities.
Satisfaction	Community	High standing.
	Service to others	Do great good.
	Accomplishment	Like no other vocation.
	Pride	Parents.

This chart should give you a concrete idea of the way in which cues may be extracted from text type material. Review the cues that were extracted, then test your retention by expanding upon the recap of the main cues listed again below.

MAIN CUES	SUB CUES	WRITE THOUGHTS RECALLED BY CUES
Requisites		
Costs		
Qualities		
Health		
Types		
Financial Reward		
Women Doctors		
Satisfaction		

The Main Cues should be memorized in a sequence using the Linking Thought method.

Example: REQUISITES COST . . . the higher the cost, the better the QUALITY. GOOD HEALTH brings all TYPES of FINANCIAL REWARDS to WOMEN DOCTORS who give SATISFACTION.

You should have recalled a great deal of the material from the story just by reading the cues presented. Some cues may bring forth more material than others. You should now check back to the article or the original chart which was prepared for you, listing the main cues and sub cues. By comparing the two, you can readily see where you may have to practice more visualization and association.

Now, you try it on your own!

The following is an article, "Should You Be a Lawyer?" Read this article, visualizing the thoughts presented as you read. Then go back and underline or write your main cue words on another sheet of paper. At the end of the article is a blank chart for you to use to list your main cues, sub cues and complete thoughts.

After you have extracted your main cues and sub cues and written them along with your thoughts expanding upon this material on the chart provided, then check your cues with the suggested ones given on the page following your chart.

"Should You Be a Lawyer?"*

By Roscoe Pound as told to Donald Robinson

Time and again, people come to me asking whether youngsters should choose the law as a calling. This is what I tell them: "It's a long, hard grind to become a lawyer, but it's worth it."

I then go on to say: "I know of no other profession that offers a young person so much opportunity for achieving wealth and prestige and, at the same time, affords him such possibilities for rendering real service to his community, his state and even his country."

In my opinion, you would be well counseled to consider the same points if you are wondering what to do with your life.

When I was a senior at the University of Nebraska—that was quite a while ago, in 1888, to be exact—I started to think very seriously of botany as a career. The reason for this is simple; I was studying under an exceptional professor of botany who had me all excited about his subject. Luckily, I asked my father what he thought of it. Father was a man of practical, good sense and he quickly convinced me that I was much better suited for law than for botany. I have been deeply grateful to him ever since.

Types of Lawyers

There are two big things for you to remember about the practice of law. One is that it provides so wide a scope for the application of a young person's native gifts.

A lawyer can be primarily an advocate—a trial man, representing his clients in court before judge and jury. Or he can be chiefly an adviser, showing clients how to stay out of court, informing them exactly what rights and what duties they have in the conduct of their affairs. Or, like many country lawyers, he can be a general practitioner and handle

---
* Copyright by New York Life Insurance Company, 1961. Reprinted by permission.

virtually every sort of legal activity. Or, if he prefers, he can concentrate just on teaching and writing about the law.

Each of these categories, of course, has its own advantages. The advocate is constantly in the public eye. The adviser, especially if he gets to be the attorney for large enterprises, may often have a far-reaching effect upon the national economy. The general practitioner can win the same warm relationships with people that a family doctor enjoys. The law teacher and writer can make an enduring name for himself.

But all of these categories have one thing in common. They will all bring a good lawyer the respect of his neighbors and associates, and, as a rule, a substantial income.

And that's not all. The good lawyer can also look forward to proffers of ranking, remunerative posts in finance or industry. The heads of many of the greatest corporations in America started out as attorneys.

Opportunity for Public Service

The second and perhaps the most significant thing for you to bear in mind about the practice of law is the chance it gives you for public service.

Lawyers have always been leaders of public life in America. Twenty-four of the signers of the Declaration of Independence were lawyers. Twenty-one of thirty-five presidents of the United States were lawyers. Congress and the state legislatures have been mainly staffed by lawyers.

At last count, no less than 32,000 lawyers were serving the federal government, states, counties and cities in varying capacities. Thousands more were holding other important government offices. The truth is that there is no better avenue to political achievement and service than the bar.

Professional Training

"But is there room for more lawyers?" People continually ask me that.

I invariably answer, "Yes."

I recognize that there are more than 260,000 lawyers in the United States today. Yet I know for a fact that there is a need for more good lawyers.

You must never forget, though, that it takes a lot of hard work to become a good lawyer. You must first spend at least three years in college; in some states, four. And you must get high grades or you won't be accepted by an accredited law school. If you are admitted to law school, you next must put in three years of still more intensive effort in order to win the cherished degree of Bachelor of Laws.

Even then your hard work is not done. You have to "pass the bar." This is an examination given by the various states to determine whether a man has a thorough knowledge and understanding of the law.

Qualities for Success

Vital as the capacity for hard work is, I don't want you to think that it is the sole prerequisite to success in the legal profession. After more than a half-century of teaching the law, I know that a young person must have certain other natural attributes, as well.

1. CHARACTER: A lawyer must have integrity, loyalty, and above all, a keen sense of honor.

Some years ago, a distinguished Chief Justice of the Supreme Court of Tennessee told his son, "No man is fit to be a lawyer who is capable of telling a lie." He was right.

2. COMMON SENSE: Millions of dollars may rest upon a lawyer's judgment. Therefore, he must be able to give solid advice.

3. SELF-RELIANCE: A lawyer must be the kind of man who can keep his head in emergency. The life, liberty, and fortunes of many people may be contingent upon his levelheadedness in a crisis.

4. PATIENCE: A lawyer frequently has to deal with rash, obstinate persons. He cannot afford to lose his temper—not if he is to persuade such people to do what is best for them.

5. ABILITY TO THINK LOGICALLY: A lawyer must be able to see through empty words and specious arguments to their true significance. The great U.S. Supreme Court Justice, Oliver Wendell Holmes, phrased it in this fashion:

"The law is not the place for the artist or the poet. The law is the calling of thinkers."

6. ABILITY TO WRITE CLEARLY: The property of a lawyer's clients may depend upon the manner in which he drafts wills, contracts, mortgages, and other legal documents. When a case goes to court, a lawyer cannot say to the judge, "Your honor, I actually meant to say it this way . . ."

It may be too late then.

7. COURAGE: To be worthy of the name, a lawyer must be ready to advocate the cases of the poor, the friendless, the oppressed, and the accused laboring under heavy burdens of prejudice, discrimination and

THE CUE METHOD OF MEMORIZING 183

public agitation, so as to assure them a fair trial and adequate presentation of their cases.

8. APTITUDE: Naturally, a youngster contemplating a legal career must also have a genuine interest in, and respect for, the law.

Cost of Schooling

You probably wish to learn now how expensive it will be to attend law school. It will be costly, that I admit. College tuition is heavy and so are law school fees. Some law schools charge as much as $1,200 a year tuition, and to that you have to add the cost of books and board.

However, that doesn't mean that the sons of poor parents cannot become lawyers. They can!

State universities, with their low tuition rates, make it possible for a young person to get a good preliminary education even if he doesn't have much money. Furthermore, many state universities have law schools for which the tuition rates are also very low, in some instances around $100 a semester. In addition, most private law schools give scholarships to youngsters with outstanding records.

And it is still perfectly feasible for a determined youngster to work his way through college and law school. I have known many, many young people who have done it and then gone on to make a big success.

What about women lawyers?

A torrent of legal briefs has gone over the bench since the first American woman was admitted to the practice of law in 1872. Today, more than 6,000 women are in active law practice. Many of these women lawyers are doing well, especially in government work. But, on the whole, the law remains a man's calling.

For the good lawyer, it is a wonderful calling. As that eminent lawyer and statesman, Joseph H. Choate, said:

"To establish justice, to maintain the rights of man, to defend the helpless and oppressed, to succor innocence, and to punish guilt, to aid in the solution of those great questions, legal and constitutional, which are constantly being evolved from the ever-varying affairs and business of men, are duties that may well challenge the best powers of man's intellect and the noblest qualities of the human heart."

This very interesting article, "Should You Be a Lawyer?" by Roscoe Pound (formerly the Dean of the Harvard Law School) should be easy for you to associate, and remember. On the blank chart which follows, write in your main cues, sub cues and thoughts for this article. When you have finished, compare your cues with the suggested ones on the subsequent page.

"Should You Be a Lawyer?"		
MAIN CUES	SUB CUES	THOUGHTS

"Should You Be a Lawyer?"
Suggested Cues

MAIN CUES	SUB CUES	THOUGHTS
Opportunity	Service	Community, state and country
	Calling	Worth the hard grind
	Wealth	
	Prestige	
Types	Advocate	Trial court—public eye
	Adviser	Rights and duties; large enterprises
	General practice	Every legal activity; relationships with people
	Teaching and writing	Enduring name
Public Service	Political	Declaration of Independence; Presidents; Congress—local—avenue to political achievement
Training	Need	260,000 lawyers
	College	Pre-Law, Law School
	Degree	Bachelor of Laws
	Bar exam	Knowledge and understanding of law
Success	Character	Integrity, loyalty, sense of honor
	Common sense	Judgment, solid advice
	Self-reliance	Levelheadedness
	Patience	Temper
	Think	Logically true significance of words
	Write	Draft legal documents
	Courage	Assure fair trial for poor, oppressed
	Aptitude	Interest, respect
Costs	Tuition	$1,200 year—state university
	Scholarships	Private law schools
Women Lawyers	First woman lawyer—	1872
	Active law practice—	6,000 government work
Quote	Justice	Establish
	Rights of man	Maintain
	Great questions	Legal and constitutional; challenge intellect

Now that you have compared your original cues with the ones presented above, the next step in remembering material of this type is to memorize the list of main cues in a perfect sequence. Then as you think of each main cue word, all the information surrounding this cue should be recalled.

Practice memorizing this list of main cues. They are the seven cues given above for the article, "Should You Be a Lawyer?" If you want to put in your linking thoughts to help build a story from these cues, then write your linking thoughts beside each cue.

CUES	LINKING THOUGHTS
Opportunity	
Types	
Public Service	
Training	
Success	
Costs	
Women Lawyers	
Quote	

Use this memory training technique whenever you need to memorize sales talks, speeches, text material, reports, articles or series of ideas. Extract the cues, recognize the total idea which each cue represents and memorize these cues. Then when you take your examination, or have to give that report or speech, the cues will come back to mind, and all the other information with them!

A FOREIGN LANGUAGE IN HALF THE TIME!

Chapter **Twelve**

You will find a foreign language useful in academic, business and social life. When you meet someone who speaks another language, say a few words in his native tongue and notice the pleased expression on his face. You will gain new friends because ideas are easily expressed through better communication.

Most students attempt to learn the vocabulary of a foreign language by tiresome repetition. Rote memorization will never bring the concentration needed to recall vocabulary, conjugations, declensions and other parts of a foreign language. Tiresome repetition alone can create a dislike for learning any language.

The application of memory training methods will make studying a foreign vocabulary interesting and fun. Proper methods will leave a deeper impression and be retained for a longer period of time. Knowing another language will give you a feeling of pleasure and accomplishment.

In this chapter, you will see how the ability to visualize, associate, classify and concentrate will enable you to learn the vocabulary of any language more quickly and easily in half the time!

The method of Linking Thoughts will be used to learn Spanish, German and French vocabularies. Since we think in English, the first step is to find a word in our own language that is similar in sound to the word in another language.

Example: English   Spanish   Link (sounds like)

world   mundo   moon

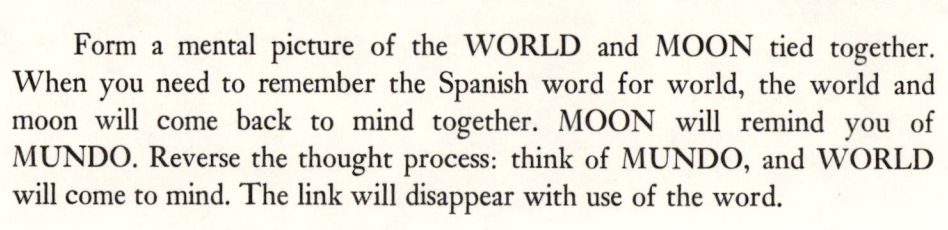

Form a mental picture of the WORLD and MOON tied together. When you need to remember the Spanish word for world, the world and moon will come back to mind together. MOON will remind you of MUNDO. Reverse the thought process: think of MUNDO, and WORLD will come to mind. The link will disappear with use of the word.

Increase Your Spanish Vocabulary

The following is a list of English words and their Spanish equivalents. There is a space between the two words for you to write your Linking Thoughts that you will use to tie the two together. Suggested Links have been given for some of these words to illustrate how your imagination and logic are used to associate the words together. Then you're on your own!

ENGLISH	LINK	SPANISH
alone	solitude	solo
amusing	diversion	divertido
answer	contest	contestacion
bread	baked in a—	pan

ENGLISH	LINK	SPANISH
business	negotiate	negocios
car	coach	coche
chair	on window sill—	sillo
city	see you, Dad	ciudad
cold	freeze	frio
country	pass through	pais
dark	obscure	obscuro
door	portal	puerto
easy	facility	facil
end	finish	fin
face	caricature	cara
field	camp on	campo
finger	digit	dido
fire	fuel	fuego
follow	sequence	sequir
foot	in pie	pie
fresh, cool	*fres*h, *coo*l	fresco
full	completely	completo
gold	ore	oro
hand		mano
hard		duro
health		salud
heart		corazon
high		alto
house		casa
husband		esposo
keep		guardar
meat		carne
mild		blando
money		dinero
noise		ruido
old		antiguo
only		unico
place		puesto

ENGLISH	LINK	SPANISH
pretty		bonita
private		propio
right		derecho
sell		vender
sing		cantar
sky		cielo
small		chico
teeth		dientes
time		tiempo
water		agua
window		ventana
year		ano
young		joven
pure		puro
minute		minuto
equal		igual
difficult		dificil
salt		sal
voice		voz
letter		letra
island		isla

You will notice that the last few words were similar in spelling, giving you a natural association. These words are called *cognates*. You will be amazed to find that you can quickly learn hundreds of Spanish words through the use of word cognates.

A New Way to Learn Spanish

Learning Spanish vocabulary is simple when association and visualization are used to tie the English and Spanish words together. This method usually requires only one impression and an occasional review to retain permanently.

Now we will discuss a way to learn hundreds of Spanish words quickly and easily. With the aid of cognates (a word that has the same origin and similar sound and spelling in another language), Spanish is easy to learn and apply. Even though there are a few exceptions, in practical use these words will be understood by any Spanish-speaking individual.

Spanish Cognate No. 1: English words ending in "ry," change to "ria" or "rio" and you have the word in Spanish.

Examples:

ENGLISH	SPANISH
vocabulary	vocabulario
glory	gloria
history	historia
dictionary	diccionario
necessary	necesario

Spanish Cognate No. 2: English nouns ending in "tion," replace with "cion" and you have the Spanish word.

Examples:

ENGLISH	SPANISH
elevation	elevación
action	acción
nation	nación
reflection	reflección
motion	moción

Spanish Cognate No. 3: English words ending in "ism," all you do is add "o."

Examples:

ENGLISH	SPANISH
optimism	optimismo
Americanism	Americanismo
pessimism	pesimismo

Spanish Cognate No. 4: Adverbs ending in "ly," change to "mente" and you have the Spanish word.

Examples:

ENGLISH	SPANISH
finally	finalmente
usually	usualmente
nationally	nacionalmente
naturally	naturalmente

Spanish Cognate No. 5: English nouns ending in "ity," replace with "idad" and you are speaking Spanish.

Examples:

ENGLISH	SPANISH
personality	personalidad
university	universidad
facility	facilidad
opportunity	oportunidad
curiosity	curiosidad

Notice other cognates as you place more and more words in your foreign vocabulary. You will find cognates in other languages as well as Spanish, so apply this method at every *oportunidad*.

For example, look at the word Mother in the following languages:

English	Mother
Latin	Mater
French	Mere
Italian	Madre
Spanish	Madre
German	Mutter
Russian	Maht
Swedish	Moder
Irish	Mathir
Sanskrit	Matr
Portuguese	Mae
Chinese	Mootyin
Japanese	Okasa*ma*
Arabic	Um

The word for sidewalk in French is *trottoir*. The word for sidewalk in Russian, although it looks very different because of the difference in the letters of the alphabet, is also sounded just like trottoir (trot-twa).

The student learning his first foreign language will know very few cognates. Whereas, if the same student masters this first language, he would have twice as many sound associations to relate to any new language he would need to learn.

This same individual, were he to continue to master more and more languages would find that by the time he comes to his fifth, sixth or seventh language, his cross associations between languages would become more obvious. He would have thousands of vocabulary words and their sounds in his mind to associate to the language he is currently studying.

Let's Learn French

Now that you have used the Linking Thought method to tie Spanish vocabulary into your mind, you will apply the same method to memorize a great number of French vocabulary words. Again, we will give you the links for some of the words, then leave you on your own to use your own individual associations.

In the following list of French words, you will notice that the English sound of the French word is as close as possible to the actual pronunciation.

Example: English   Link   French (sounds like)

cabbage   shoe   chou   (shoe)

Use your imagination and picture a huge CABBAGE stuffed into a SHOE. When you think of CABBAGE again, the SHOE will also appear in your mental picture, to remind you of CHOU.

ENGLISH	LINK	FRENCH	WORD SOUND
chicken	poultry	poulet	pool-ay
frozen	jelly	gelee	zh-lay
odor	perfume	parfum	par-fum
print	stamp	estampe	es-tamp
profit	lucrative	lucre	lukr
pauper	miserable	miserable	meez-ay-rah-bl
ruins	remains	debris	day-bree
sand	sable in sand	sable	sah-bl
anger	cool with air	colere	koh-lair
to bind up	band	bander	ban-der
boot		botte	bott
compel	oblige	obliger	ob-lee-zhay
day	soup du jour	jour	zhoor
dream	reverie	rever	rehv-ay
future	avenue	avenir	ahv-neer

ENGLISH	LINK	FRENCH	WORD SOUND
freshness	_____	fraicheur	fraysh-ur
hook	_____	crochet	krosh-ay
to heap up	_____	entasser	on-tass-ay
joy	_____	plaisir	plez-eer
journal	_____	gazette	gah-zett
jacket	_____	veston	vest-on
be late	_____	tarder	tar-day
my	_____	ma	mah
notice	_____	remarquer	re-mark-ay
pig	_____	porc	por-k
quick	_____	vite	veet
ribbon	_____	ruban	ru-baun
to read	_____	lire	leer
soft	_____	tendre	taun-dr
to speak	_____	parler	par-lay
to sleep	_____	dormir	dor-meer
safety	_____	securite	say-kur-ee-tay
self-praise	_____	vanterie	vant-ay-ree
small	_____	mignon	meen-yon
tobacco	_____	tobac	tab-ah
triumph	_____	triomphe	tree-onf
tunnel	_____	tunnel	tun-nel
thin	_____	maigre	meh-gr
tint	_____	teindre	tain-dr
to understand	_____	comprendre	kom-pron-dr
to unite	_____	unir	u-neer
voice	_____	voix	vwa
visit	_____	visite	veez-eet
wild	_____	sauvage	soh-vahzh
you	_____	vous	voo

Review these French words you have just memorized and have someone test you. When learning any foreign language, keep up with the vocabulary by memorizing 10 or more new words each day. Remember: before memorizing any new foreign vocabulary words, always review the vocabulary words you memorized the day before.

Let's Learn German

Linking Thoughts will be used to associate German vocabulary in your mind. More imagination will be used, because German is a more difficult language than either Spanish or French. Also, there may be fewer cognates than you have noticed in the other two languages. With imagination and a good visual picture to link the English word to its German equivalent, it will be easy for you to learn German vocabulary.

Example: English   Link   German (sounds like)

potato   cart full of potatoes   kartoffel (kahr-tof-fel)

KARTOFFEL sounds like CART-FULL. To tie KARTOFFEL and POTATO together visualize a CART-FULL of POTATOES.

Practice on the following list of German words. Remember to use your imagination to tie the German word to its English equivalent.

ENGLISH	LINK	GERMAN	WORD SOUND
chair	stool	stuhl	shtool
desk	pulp wood	pult	pult
head	cup	kopf	kopf
meat	flesh	fleisch	fly-sch
river	flows	Fluss	floos
blossom	flower	flor	flohr
breakfast	fruit stuck	fruhstuck	fru-shtuck
breathe	how can	hauchen	how-ken
box	load	lade	lahd-erh
before	fore	vor	for
chin	————	kinn	kin
outside wall	lawn mower	mauer	mower
closet	I bought	abort	ah-bought
cannon	————	kanone	kahn-ohn-erh
capture	————	fangen	fahng-n

ENGLISH	LINK	GERMAN	WORD SOUND
dealer	_____	handler	hand-dler
dark	_____	dunkel	doon-kel
fleet, navy	_____	flotte	flot-tuh
free	_____	frei	frei
fortune	_____	habe	hah-ber
fever	_____	fieber	fee-ber
gum	_____	gummie	gommee
glass	_____	glas	glahs
greyhound	_____	windhund	winnt-hoont
handle	_____	handhabe	hahnt-hahb-n
island	_____	eiland	i-lahnt
kiss	_____	kuss	koos
kitchen	_____	kuche	ku-chuh
knife	_____	messer	mes-ser
money	_____	geld	gelt
milk	_____	milch	milch
mirror	_____	spiegel	shpeeg-l
on	_____	auf	owf
please	_____	bitte	bit-tuh
to put	_____	setzen	sets-n
round	_____	rund	roont
ride	_____	ritt	rit
red	_____	rot	roht
sparrow	_____	sperling	shpayr-ling
silver	_____	silber	sil-ber
talk	_____	sage	sah-gerh
treasure	_____	hort	hort
upward	_____	herauf	hair-owf
unlucky	_____	fatal	faht-ahl
upstairs	_____	oben	oh-ben

Let's Take a Test

Test your retention for the words that you have just learned in Spanish, French and German. Look at the English word, think quickly of your association, then write the foreign word next to it. Ready? Begin!

ENGLISH	SPANISH
bread	_____
car	_____
cold	_____
dark	_____
door	_____
end	_____
field	_____
follow	_____
foot	_____
gold	_____
meat	_____
old	_____
sing	_____
window	_____
hard	_____
chair	_____

ENGLISH	FRENCH
cabbage	_____
frozen	_____
odor	_____
profit	_____
ruins	_____
hook	_____
joy	_____
jacket	_____
quick	_____
soft	_____
to sleep	_____
small	_____
to speak	_____
wild	_____
to read	_____
chicken	_____

ENGLISH	GERMAN
desk	_____
river	_____
box	_____
mirror	_____
upstairs	_____
glass	_____
closet	_____
head	_____
chair	_____
breakfast	_____
dealer	_____
dark	_____
fortune	_____
greyhound	_____
talk	_____
please	_____

Your Score _____

When learning any new language, first look for cognates or similarities between the word in the other language and the word in English. If no obvious relationship exists, then use your imagination and ability to visualize two ideas going together. You can associate the English word with its equivalent by working with either the sound or the spelling of the other word.

Remember to apply the techniques discussed in this chapter and make a mental picture such as the ones illustrated. Then you, too, can cut your study time in half when learning any foreign language . . . and most important, bring back the information when you need it again. These words will be where they should be—at your fingertips!

NOTE: Use a 3 x 5 card system. Write the English word on the front of the card and the foreign word on the back of the card. Look at the English word and instantly recall the foreign equivalent. Look at the foreign word and recall the English.

LET'S TEST YOUR MEMORY POWER

Chapter **Thirteen**

Now that you understand various memory methods and how they are applied, the next step is additional practice and application. In this final section you will be presented with different subject matter to memorize, applying various systems that you have learned in this course. Continue to practice and you will become proficient at applying the memory methods in your business and social life.

I have chosen several examples to start you on your way. For instance, you will apply your Linking Thought method to learn all the state capitals as well as capitals of countries throughout the world.

To remember all the Presidents of the United States or all the world leaders in a particular era, you would apply our system of tying a series of cues together. If you wish this information memorized in a numerical sequence, then you would apply your Visual Key Words to this particular subject matter.

To remember historical dates or the numerical factors that are associated with atomic elements you will apply numerical words, which, when translated by the Numerical Alphabet, will give you the exact number that you need to remember.

If you wanted to remember all the symbols on the Stock Exchange, the initial system of remembering plus Linking Thoughts will be applied.

If you have difficulty spelling, then with a little imagination and application of one or more memory systems, you can master hundreds of different words that may have troubled you in the past.

To increase your vocabulary, again use a little imagination and you can associate hundreds, or even thousands, of words and their definitions together.

If you volunteered to publicly recite a passage verbatim or just for your own self-improvement wanted to memorize the Optimist Creed, your Cue System or Visual Keys can be applied.

The most important thing to keep in mind: You now have memory methods that will work for you in any area of learning whenever you need them.

Remember—motivation, that is, "I want to learn . . . I see the benefits" *plus* the confidence, "I can, I will and I shall learn," should be in the uppermost part of your mind at all times.

With this positive attitude in mind, proceed to memorize all of the material in this final section. You will not only be pleased with the additional knowledge that you will possess, but you will also see that more and more practice will only strengthen the systems you now possess and make your mind the storehouse of knowledge that it was intended to be.

Remember the Presidents

We will remember the Presidents of the United States by using our Linking Thought method. Words that are similar in sound or spelling are substituted for the Presidents' names, as follows:

PRESIDENT	SUBSTITUTE WORD
Washington	Washington
Adams	Adam
Jefferson	Jeff
Madison	made
Monroe	money
J. Q. Adams	adventure
Jackson	Jacksonville
Van Buren	bureau
Harrison	hairy
Tyler	tile
Polk	poker
Taylor	table
Fillmore	fill-more
Pierce	pierced
Buchanan	by a cannon
Lincoln	Lincoln
Johnson	jaunted
Grant	grand
Hayes	haze
Garfield	garden
Arthur	arbor
Cleveland	cleaving
Harrison	hurriedly
Cleveland	clever
McKinley	mockingbird
Roosevelt	roses
Taft	tuft
Wilson	willows
Harding	hardly
Coolidge	cool
Hoover	hues
F. D. Roosevelt	rose
Truman	true man
Eisenhower	eyes
Kennedy	Ken
Johnson	Johnson

NOTE: There are 36 presidents listed and illustrated, and the latest ones are Nixon, Ford, Carter and Reagan.

Nixon	St. Nick-on
Ford	automobile
Carter	a cart
Reagan	Ray Gun

Make up your own linking thoughts to represent these presidents.

These words that represent the Presidents' names can be linked together to form sentences that tell a story. You can see the reasoning from word to word by noticing that there is a who, what, where, when and why relationship that keeps these cues in a perfect sequence. As an example:

STORY	LOGICAL THOUGHTS (ASK YOURSELF)
In Washington	(who was there?)
Adam and Jeff	(what did they do?)
made money	(for what?)
for an adventure	(where?)
to Jacksonville.	(what happened next?)
At the bureau,	(what did they do?)
they put hairy tile	(where?)
on the poker table.	(what happened next?)
They filled more holes	(how did they get there?)
pierced by a cannon	(when?)
when Lincoln jaunted	(where?)
through the grand haze.	(scene changes)
On the garden arbor	(what's happening?)
cleaving hurriedly was	(what?)
a clever mockingbird.	(now what?)
The roses were tuft	(where?)
near the willows;	(and what happened?)
hardly any cool hues rose from	(what?)
the true man's eyes when he	(did what?)
saw Ken Johnson.	

Read the entire story twice. Remember to visualize as you read. At this point it is not important to think of the Presidents' names. Concentrate on remembering the story.

In *WASHINGTON*, *ADAM* and *JEFF MADE MONEY* for an *ADVENTURE* to *JACKSONVILLE*. At the *BUREAU*, they put *HAIRY TILE* on the *POKER TABLE* to *FILL MORE* holes *PIERCED BY A CANNON* when *LINCOLN JAUNTED* through the *GRAND HAZE*. On the *GARDEN ARBOR*, *CLEAVING HURRIEDLY*, was a *CLEVER MOCKINGBIRD*. The *ROSES* were *TUFT* near the *WILLOWS*; *HARDLY* any *COOL HUES ROSE* from the *TRUE MAN'S EYES* when he saw *KEN JOHNSON*.

Notice that as you come to each word in italic caps in the story above, these words will remind you of each President's name in correct order. See the next page for a test of your retention of the Presidents of the United States.

Test Your Retention

Now that you have read the story twice, write the names of all the Presidents. Recall the story, writing the name of each President as you come to the word that reminds you of the President's name.

_____   _____
_____   _____
_____   _____
_____   _____
_____   _____
_____   _____
_____   _____
_____   _____
_____   _____
_____   _____
_____   _____
_____   _____
_____   _____
_____   _____
_____   _____
_____   _____
_____   _____
_____   _____
_____   _____

Memorize the Presidents in Numerical Order

As a practical exercise, memorize the names of the Presidents by using your Visual Key Words. This will enable you to recall them by number in sequence or out of sequence, such as the 6th President, the 19th, the 23rd, etc. Use your Visual Key Words from 1 through 36 to memorize their names. Tie the name of each President to the corresponding Key Word. As an example, Key Word HUT and Washington; HEN and Adams; HAM and Jefferson; MATCH and JOHNSON.

NO.	KEY WORD	PRESIDENT	ASSOCIATION
1.	HUT	Washington	A *ton of washing* beside the *hut*.
2.	HEN	Adams	See a *hen* with a HUGE *adam's* apple.
3.	HAM	Jefferson	The favorite food of *Jeff's son* is *ham*.
4.	HARE	Madison	The *hare* is *mad at his son*.
5.	HILL	Monroe	*Money* rolling down the *hill*.
6.	JAY	J. Q. Adams	*Jay* reminds you of *J. Q. Adams*.
7.	HOOK	Jackson	Put your *jacket* on the *hook*.
8.	HIVE	Van Buren	The *hive* is on a *bureau in a van*.
9.	APE	Harrison	The hairy *ape* has a *hairy son*.
10.	TOES	Tyler	Rub your *toes* on the *tile*.

Continue on your own. Write your associations in the spaces provided.

11.	TIDE	Polk	_____
12.	TIN	Taylor	_____
13.	TAM	Fillmore	_____
14.	TIRE	Pierce	_____
15.	TAIL	Buchanan	_____
16.	TISSUE	Lincoln	_____
17.	TAG	Johnson	_____
18.	TAFFY	Grant	_____
19.	TUB	Hayes	_____
20.	NOSE	Garfield	_____
21.	NET	Arthur	_____

LET'S TEST YOUR MEMORY POWER 205

NO.	KEY WORD	PRESIDENT	ASSOCIATION
22.	NUN	Cleveland	_____
23.	NAME	Harrison	_____
24.	NERO	Cleveland	_____
25.	NAIL	McKinley	_____
26.	NICHE	Roosevelt	_____
27.	NECK	Taft	_____
28.	NAVY	Wilson	_____
29.	KNOB	Harding	_____
30.	MICE	Coolidge	_____
31.	MAT	Hoover	_____
32.	MOON	Roosevelt	_____
33.	MIMEO	Truman	_____
34.	MARE	Eisenhower	_____
35.	MAIL	Kennedy	_____
36.	MATCH	Johnson	_____

37. MIKE-Nixon_____ 38. MUFF-Ford_____ 39. MOP-Carter_____ 40. RICE-Reagan_____

After you have written all of your associations, review them once more, visualizing as you review, then test your retention.

Test Your Retention

Next to the Key Words below, write the name of the President that you associated with each Key Word.

KEY WORD	PRESIDENT
1. HUT	_____
2. HEN	_____
3. HAM	_____
4. HARE	_____
5. HILL	_____
6. JAY	_____
7. HOOK	_____
8. HIVE	_____
9. APE	_____

KEY WORD	PRESIDENT
10. TOES	_____
11. TIDE	_____
12. TIN	_____
13. TAM	_____
14. TIRE	_____
15. TAIL	_____
16. TISSUE	_____
17. TAG	_____
18. TAFFY	_____
19. TUB	_____
20. NOSE	_____
21. NET	_____
22. NUN	_____
23. NAME	_____
24. NERO	_____
25. NAIL	_____
26. NICHE	_____
27. NECK	_____
28. NAVY	_____
29. KNOB	_____
30. MICE	_____
31. MAT	_____
32. MOON	_____
33. MIMEO	_____
34. MARE	_____
35. MAIL	_____
36. MATCH	_____
37. MIKE	_____
38. MUFF	_____
39. MOP	_____
40. RICE	_____

Number Correct _____

On the next three pages, you will find pictures of the first 36 Presidents. Study these pictures as an exercise in observation of their facial features and characteristics. When recalling their names, visualize their faces. Then go on to the next page where you will learn how to memorize the date that each President entered office.

Presidents of the United States

1. **George Washington**–1789
2. **John Adams**–1797 
3. **Thomas Jefferson**–1801 
4. **James Madison**–1809 
5. **James Monroe**–1817 
6. **John Q. Adams**–1825 
7. **Andrew Jackson**–1829 
8. **Martin Van Buren**–1837 
9. **William H. Harrison**–1841 
10. **John Tyler**–1841 
11. **James Polk**–1845 
12. **Zachary Taylor**–1849

Presidents of the United States

13. **Millard Fillmore**–1850

14. **Franklin Pierce**–1853

15. **James Buchanan**–1857

16. **Abraham Lincoln**–1861

21. **Chester Arthur**–1881

22. **Grover Cleveland**–1885

23. **Benjamin Harrison**–1889

24. **Grover Cleveland**–1893

29. **Warren Harding**–1921

30. **Calvin Coolidge**–1923

31. **Herbert Hoover**–1929

32. **Franklin D. Roosevelt**–19

LET'S TEST YOUR MEMORY POWER   209

Presidents of the United States

17. **Andrew Johnson**–1865 
18. **Ulysses S. Grant**–1869 
19. **Rutherford Hayes**–1877 
20. **James Garfield**–1881

25. **William McKinley**–1897 
26. **Theodore Roosevelt**–1901 
27. **William H. Taft**–1909 
28. **Woodrow Wilson**–1913

33. **Harry S. Truman**–1945
34. **Dwight Eisenhower**–1953 
35. **John F. Kennedy**–1961 
36. **Lyndon B. Johnson**–1963

Presidents and Year They Entered Office

You can remember the year that each President entered office by using numerical words to represent the dates. By classification, we can easily remember that the first two Presidents entered office in the 1700's. Jefferson was the first President in the 1800's. Theodore Roosevelt was the first President in the 1900's. Therefore, the millenium and the hundred year in the dates are disregarded because you only need to remember the last two digits. Using the Numerical Alphabet, we will choose words to represent these numbers.

The same words substituted for the Presidents' names in the paragraph just learned will be used once again: MADE for Madison, MONEY for Monroe, BUREAU for Van Buren, etc. Associate the numerical words with them. When translated back into numbers according to the Numerical Alphabet, the words will give the year when that President took office.

PRESIDENT	YEAR	WORD	ASSOCIATION
Washington (Washington)	1789	fib	Washington never told a FIB.
Adams (Adam)	1797	big	Adam was a BIG man.
Jefferson (Jeff)	1801	city	Jefferson CITY, Missouri.
Madison (made)	1809	soup	Made SOUP.
Monroe (money)	1817	dig	DIG for money.
J. Q. Adams (adventure)	1825	Nile	Adventure down the NILE.
Jackson (Jacksonville)	1829	nab	NAB him in Jacksonville.
Van Buren (bureau)	1837	mug	See the MUG on the bureau.
Harrison (hairy)	1841	rat	A hairy RAT.
Tyler (tile)	1841	road	Tile the ROAD.

Continue on your own. Write your associations below.

Polk (poker)	1845	royal	_____
Taylor (table)	1849	rap	_____
Fillmore (fill more)	1850	laws	_____

LET'S TEST YOUR MEMORY POWER

PRESIDENT	YEAR	WORD	ASSOCIATION
Pierce (pierce)	1853	lime	_____
Buchanan (by-cannon)	1857	log	_____
Lincoln (Lincoln)	1861	shot	_____
Johnson (jaunted)	1865	agile	_____
Grant (grand)	1869	ship	_____
Hayes (haze)	1877	cook	_____
Garfield (garden)	1881	food	_____
Arthur (arbor)	1881	foot	_____
Cleveland (cleaving)	1885	fly	_____
Harrison (hurriedly)	1889	fob	_____
Cleveland (clever)	1893	poem	_____
McKinley (mockingbird)	1897	peck	_____
T. Roosevelt (roses)	1901	seed	_____
Taft (tuft)	1909	wasp	_____
Wilson (willows)	1913	autumn	_____
Harding (hardly)	1921	nut	_____
Coolidge (cool)	1923	numb	_____
Hoover (hues)	1929	nip	_____
F. D. Roosevelt (rose)	1933	mummy	_____
Truman (true man)	1945	roll	_____
Eisenhower (eyes)	1953	limb	_____
Kennedy (Ken)	1961	jet	_____
Johnson (Johnson)	1963	jam	_____
Nixon (St. Nick)	1969	ship	_____
Ford (automobile)	1974	car	_____
Cart (cart)	1977	cake	_____
Reagan (ray gun)	1981	fat	_____

Now that you have associated the word that represents the year that each of the Presidents entered office, turn the page and test your retention.

Test Yourself

The following is a list of the Presidents of the United States. Beside each name, write the numerical word which you associated with that President, then write the year that the numerical word represents.

PRESIDENT	WORD	YEAR TOOK OFFICE
Washington		
Adams		
Jefferson		
Madison		
Monroe		
J. Q. Adams		
Jackson		
Van Buren		
Harrison		
Tyler		
Polk		
Taylor		
Fillmore		
Pierce		
Buchanan		
Lincoln		
Johnson		
Grant		
Hayes		
Garfield		
Arthur		
Cleveland (1st term)		
Harrison		
Cleveland (2nd term)		
McKinley		
T. Roosevelt		
Taft		
Wilson		
Harding		

PRESIDENT	WORD	YEAR TOOK OFFICE
Coolidge	_____	_____
Hoover	_____	_____
F. D. Roosevelt	_____	_____
Truman	_____	_____
Eisenhower	_____	_____
Kennedy	_____	_____
Johnson	_____	_____

NUMBER CORRECT _____

How to Remember Historical Dates

Important dates and events have marked the development of our civilization. We should know these historical facts so that we can be well-informed individuals.

In school, we learned dates such as 1776 by rote. With a poem, we all learned the association for Columbus and the year he discovered America:

> "In fourteen hundred and ninety-two,
> Columbus sailed the ocean blue."

Now that you are more aware of methods, you can use observation to notice the logical progression of numbers. As an example: 753 B.C., the legendary date that the Seven Hills of Rome were founded by Romulus and Remus. The Seven Hills gives you a logical association for the beginning number "7" of the date. Two brothers, so subtract "2" from "7" = 5. Subtract "2" again = 3. This gives the date 753 B.C.

Very simple! But how do we remember that Napoleon was defeated at Waterloo in 1815, that the Monroe Doctrine was signed in 1823? The reason most number combinations are difficult to remember is because they lack meaning.

With our memory training methods, any historical date is easily learned and retained. We use our Numerical Alphabet to make a word that will represent the date. Then we use Linking Thoughts to tie the word to the historical event. This word, when translated back into a number, always gives us the correct date.

When recalling the date, we would not be 1,000 years off. For a year that contains four digits, it is not necessary to translate the millennium (or thousand) year. Eliminating the number one, we only need to remember the three-digit number that remains.

Example: The Battle of Cowpens in 1781.

We already know that we do not translate the first digit. To represent the "781," we can use a word such as *GIFT*. Picture two COWS in a Pen battling over a GIFT. BATTLE OF COWPENS—*GIFT*—1781.

Memorize the historical dates which follow. First the event is listed, then the year in which it occurred, then the word that represents the date. You will notice that we have used some words that have more than three consonants. Since we need only three numbers, we translate the first three consonants, and disregard the remaining consonants. As an example: Buddha was born in 563 B.C. *OIL–SHAMPOO* is the word that represents 563. We know that we only need the 563, so we do not translate the "P" in shampoo. Picture Buddha taking an *OIL–SHAMPOO*.

LET'S TEST YOUR MEMORY POWER

HISTORICAL EVENT	DATE	WORD
Burning of Rome.	64 A.D.	*ch*a*r*
Marco Polo reached China.	1275	u*ncl*e
Joan of Arc at height of her fame.	1429	*r*ai*nb*ow
Gutenberg Bible was printed.	1456	*r*e*l*i*g*ion
Ponce de Leon named Florida.	1513	*l*ou*d-m*outh
Magellan discovered Philippine Islands.	1521	i*sl*a*nd*
Louisiana Purchase.	1803	*h*ea*v*y-*s*u*m*
British burned Washington, D.C.	1814	*v*o*t*e*r*
Napoleon defeated at Waterloo.	1815	*f*a*t*a*l*
Monroe Doctrine signed.	1823	*v*e*n*o*m*
Erie Canal completed.	1825	*f*u*nn*e*l*
Bicycle invented by MacMillan.	1842	*fr*ie*nd*
U.S. purchased Alaska from Russia.	1867	*f*i*sh-h*oo*k*
Admiral Peary reached North Pole.	1909	*p*a*ss*por*t*

Cover the page and take a test of your retention.

Test Yourself

Test your retention of the historical dates which you have just memorized. First write the numerical word which you associated, then translate that word into the historical date which it represents.

HISTORICAL EVENT	WORD	DATE
Burning of Rome.	_____	_____
Marco Polo reached China.	_____	_____
Joan of Arc at height of her fame.	_____	_____
Gutenberg Bible printed.	_____	_____
Ponce de Leon named Florida.	_____	_____
Magellan discovered Philippine Islands.	_____	_____
Louisiana Purchase.		
British burned Washington, D.C.	_____	_____

HISTORICAL EVENT	WORD	DATE
Napoleon defeated at Waterloo.	_____	_____
Monroe Doctrine signed.	_____	_____
Erie Canal completed.	_____	_____
Bicycle invented by MacMillan.	_____	_____
United States purchased Alaska.	_____	_____
Admiral Peary reached North Pole.	_____	_____

NUMBER CORRECT _____

Memorize the State Capitals

In elementary school, most students memorize all the capitals of the United States. Yet, by the time they leave high school, few capitals are retained in mind. How many do you remember?

Take a Geography Test

There are 50 states in the United States of America. Take the following retention test on just a few state capitals. Write the capital of the state of:

Connecticut	_____	Maine	_____
Illinois	_____	Kentucky	_____
Washington	_____	Tennessee	_____
Maryland	_____	Delaware	_____
Michigan	_____	New Mexico	_____
Minnesota	_____	South Dakota	_____
Missouri	_____	Ohio	_____
South Carolina	_____	Nevada	_____
Pennsylvania	_____	New Hampshire	_____
Wisconsin	_____	Alaska	_____

Cover the page and check your answers with the correct answers.

LET'S TEST YOUR MEMORY POWER   217

Answers to State Capitals Test

   The correct answers to the geography test in the preceding list are given below. Check your answers and write the number you answered correctly.

STATE	CAPITAL	STATE	CAPITAL
Connecticut	Hartford	Maine	Augusta
Illinois	Springfield	Kentucky	Frankfort
Washington	Olympia	Tennessee	Nashville
Maryland	Annapolis	Delaware	Dover
Michigan	Lansing	New Mexico	Santa Fe
Minnesota	St. Paul	South Dakota	Pierre
Missouri	Jefferson City	Ohio	Columbus
South Carolina	Columbia	Nevada	Carson City
Pennsylvania	Harrisburg	New Hampshire	Concord
Wisconsin	Madison	Alaska	Juneau

NUMBER CORRECT _____

You can easily and quickly memorize all 50 state capitals by using our Linking Thought method to develop a link between the state and its capital.

Example: The capital of Maine is Augusta. To remember that Augusta is the capital of the state of Maine, visualize a "GUST OF" wind blowing down MAIN street. Notice the illustration below.

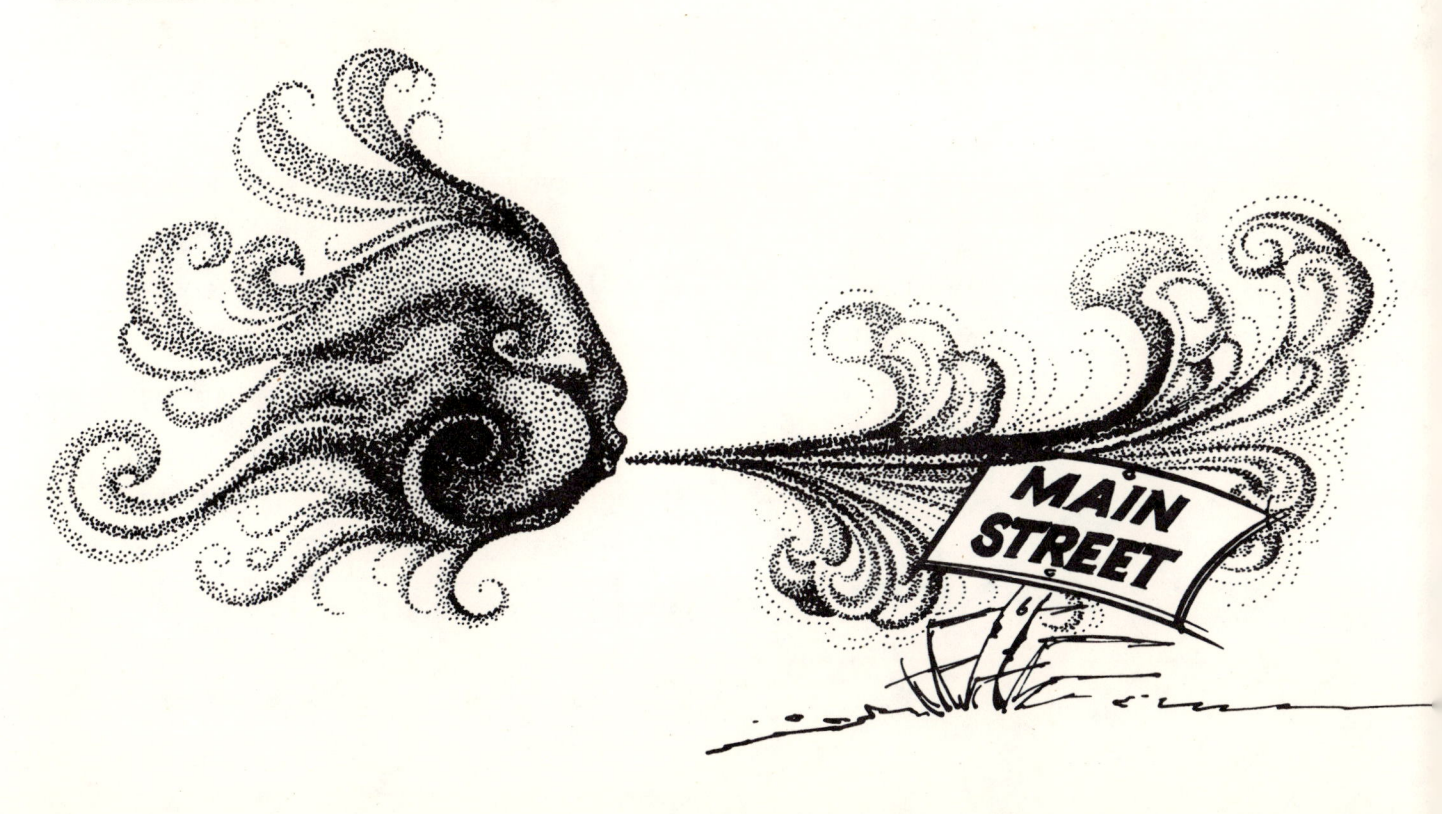

The following is a list of all 50 states, their capitals and the association which you could make to tie them into your mind permanently.

STATE	ASSOCIATION	CAPITAL
ALABAMA	*Ali-Baba* rode into the *mountains*.	Montgomery
ALASKA	*Do you know* the capital of *Alaska?*	Juneau
ARIZONA	*Phoebe* travels by *air*.	Phoenix
ARKANSAS	The *ark* is *rocking*.	Little Rock
CALIFORNIA	*Cal* bought a *sack of mementoes*.	Sacramento
COLORADO	It's *cold* in the *den*.	Denver
CONNECTICUT	*Connie* set her *heart on a Ford*.	Hartford
DELAWARE	*Della dove* into the Delaware River.	Dover
FLORIDA	*Floors* in a *tall house*.	Tallahassee
GEORGIA	King *George* sails on the *Atlantic* Ocean.	Atlanta
HAWAII	Take your *honey, Lulu*, to *Hawaii*.	Honolulu
IDAHO	The *Idaho* potatoes are *boiling*.	Boise
ILLINOIS	*Ill noises spring in the field*.	Springfield
INDIANA	The *Indians* raced at *Indianapolis*.	Indianapolis
IOWA	*I owe da money*.	Des Moines
KANSAS	*Can this* be *tapioca* pudding?	Topeka
KENTUCKY	*Ken* ate *frankfurters* in Kentucky.	Frankfort
LOUISIANA	*Louise and Ana* bought *better rouge*.	Baton Rouge
MAINE	A *gust of wind* down *Main* St.	Augusta
MARYLAND	A *merry land* is a *navy place*.	Annapolis
MASSACHUSETTS	*Mask* the *Boston* terrier.	Boston
MICHIGAN	*Michigan* loves to hear *Len sing*.	Lansing
MINNESOTA	*Minnie* saw *St. Paul's* Cathedral.	St. Paul
MISSISSIPPI	Little *misses* play *jacks*.	Jackson
MISSOURI	He *mowed Jefferson's* lawn.	Jefferson City

LET'S TEST YOUR MEMORY POWER

STATE	ASSOCIATION	CAPITAL
MONTANA	*Helen mounted her tan* pony.	Helena
NEBRASKA	*New brass* on *Lincoln's* statue.	Lincoln
NEVADA	Kit *Carson* said, "*No water?*"	Carson City
N.H.	A *new hamster* was *conked by a cord.*	Concord
N.J.	Put a *new jersey tent* on the ground.	Trenton
N.M.	*New Mexico* raised *Santa's pay.*	Santa Fe
N.Y.	We're *all bound* for *New York.*	Albany
N.C.	*Northern car lines* lead to the *rally.*	Raleigh
N.D.	*Bismark* was a *Nordic.*	Bismarck
OHIO	*Columbus* shouted, "*O-HI-O . . .* land!"	Columbus
OKLAHOMA	There are *oak homes in the city.*	Oklahoma City
OREGON	Sell 'em *ore* in Oregon.	Salem
PENNSYLVANIA	*Harry's bird* can bring *pencils.*	Harrisburg
RHODE ISLAND	We *rowed to the island* for *provisions.*	Providence
S.C.	*Columbia,* the gem of *South Carolina.*	Columbia
S.D.	*Pierre* went *South in the day coach.*	Pierre
TENNESSEE	*Bashful* boy plays *tennis by the sea.*	Nashville
TEXAS	The *taxi* is an *Austin.*	Austin
UTAH	*You, Pa,* see the *salt lake.*	Salt Lake City
VERMONT	The *vermin* left a *mound of peelings.*	Montpelier
VIRGINIA	*Virginia* married a *rich man.*	Richmond
W. VIRGINIA	*West, Virginia* danced the *Charleston.*	Charleston
WASHINGTON	The *Olympics* are held in *Washington.*	Olympia
WISCONSIN	*Whiskey* will make you *mad, son.*	Madison
WYOMING	*Shy Ann* was always *whining.*	Cheyenne

When you have made good, concrete mental pictures of the states and their capitals together, turn the page and test your retention.

Test Yourself

The following is a list of the 50 states. Beside each one, write the name of the capital of that state. Remember to look at the name of the state, then ask yourself, "What did I associate with it?" Then write the name of the capital.

STATE	CAPITAL
MAINE	_____
ARKANSAS	_____
COLORADO	_____
FLORIDA	_____
OHIO	_____
TEXAS	_____
NEW YORK	_____
VIRGINIA	_____
ALASKA	_____
MISSISSIPPI	_____
WASHINGTON	_____
ALABAMA	_____
SO. DAKOTA	_____
DELAWARE	_____
HAWAII	_____
INDIANA	_____
LOUISIANA	_____
MASSACHUSETTS	_____
NEW JERSEY	_____
MINNESOTA	_____
KENTUCKY	_____
MARYLAND	_____
GEORGIA	_____
IDAHO	_____
MISSOURI	_____
NEVADA	_____
ILLINOIS	_____
CALIFORNIA	_____

STATE	CAPITAL
CONNECTICUT	_____
IOWA	_____
KANSAS	_____
WYOMING	_____
NEW HAMPSHIRE	_____
NO. DAKOTA	_____
SO. CAROLINA	_____
OKLAHOMA	_____
PENNSYLVANIA	_____
TENNESSEE	_____
VERMONT	_____
W. VIRGINIA	_____
NEW MEXICO	_____
OREGON	_____
NO. CAROLINA	_____
RHODE ISLAND	_____
UTAH	_____
MONTANA	_____
NEBRASKA	_____
ARIZONA	_____
WISCONSIN	_____

NUMBER CORRECT _____

Use this same Linking Thought method to memorize capitals of countries throughout the world. You should find that as you practice using the techniques together with imagination, your speed in making associations will increase. Your retention will be greater as you practice. Soon the technique will become an automatic process.

Remember World Capitals

Remembering capitals of countries all around the world is easy when we use our Linking Thought method. We just learned the capitals of the United States. Now let's apply the same technique to memorize capitals of countries.

Example: The capital of Turkey is Ankara. ANKARA sounds like "anchor," and TURKEY is obvious. Picture a TURKEY with an ANCHOR around its neck. TURKEY—ANKARA.

Associate the following world capitals in the same manner. Use your imagination.

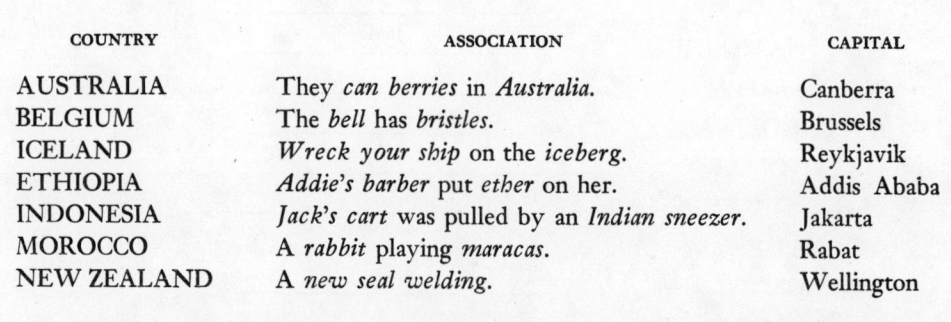

COUNTRY	ASSOCIATION	CAPITAL
AUSTRALIA	They *can berries* in *Australia*.	Canberra
BELGIUM	The *bell* has *bristles*.	Brussels
ICELAND	*Wreck your ship* on the *iceberg*.	Reykjavik
ETHIOPIA	*Addie's barber* put *ether* on her.	Addis Ababa
INDONESIA	*Jack's cart* was pulled by an *Indian sneezer*.	Jakarta
MOROCCO	A *rabbit* playing *maracas*.	Rabat
NEW ZEALAND	A *new seal welding*.	Wellington

When you are reading newspapers or magazines, listening to the radio or viewing television, pay close attention to facts about countries in the distant corners of the earth. Associate the information given about the country in your mind. You will quickly become a well informed individual and a more interesting conversationalist.

ADDITIONAL PRACTICAL APPLICATION

Chapter **Fourteen**

How to Increase Your Vocabulary

Vocabulary is easy to remember when imagination is applied to associate the word to its meaning. The same technique you learned in the Foreign Language Section will be applied to your English vocabulary.

Example: Noisome means foul smelling. Use your imagination and visualize someone holding a skunk and saying, "Does this FOUL SMELL ANNOY SOME?" NOISOME—FOUL SMELLING.

Associate the following words with their definitions. Remember to use your imagination. Ask yourself, what does it sound like? Develop a linking thought between the word and its definition and you will find that when you think of the word again, the definition will be tied to it.

WORD	LINK: SOUNDS LIKE	MEANING
ALTERCATION	The *alteration* caused a . . .	Dispute, Argument
BRANDISH	Shake *brandy* over a *dish*.	Shake or Wave
BLAND	*Blend* it and it becomes . . .	Mild, Gentle
INNOCUOUS	*Inoculation* is . . .	Harmless
INSIPID	*When he sipped*, the drink was . . .	Dull, Tasteless
INTREPID	*In he tripped*, but he was . . .	Fearless
SLAKE	Quench your thirst by the *s-lake*.	Quench
TENACIOUS	*Tennis shoes* hold fast to the ground.	Hold Fast
TEPID	The *teapot is* . . .	Lukewarm

Test Yourself

Test your retention of the vocabulary words and meanings which you have just associated. Next to the words below, write the meanings. When you look at the word, your linking thought should come back to mind, reminding you of the meaning.

WORD	MEANING
ALTERCATION	_____
BRANDISH	_____
BLAND	_____
INNOCUOUS	_____
INSIPID	_____
INTREPID	_____
NOISOME	_____
SLAKE	_____
TENACIOUS	_____
TEPID	_____

NUMBER CORRECT _____

Use this technique whenever you wish to associate the definition with a new word in your vocabulary. You can work on your vocabulary every day and even if you only learn *one* new word each day, consistently, you will have increased your vocabulary by 365 words at the end of one year. Think how rapidly you can increase your vocabulary if you learn 10 new words each day!

When you are reading and run across a word that you cannot define, don't pass it by! It may hold the meaning of an entire section or article. Go to your dictionary and look up the definition. Then associate the meaning with the word. Your reading will be more meaningful and you will use these new words in conversation and correspondence with ease and confidence.

How to Improve Your Spelling

In school you learned the little verse, "I before E, except after C, or when sounded like A as in neighbor and weigh." This verse was created to help you remember how to spell! Most people remember this and use it for the words to which it applies. You can remember also how to spell correctly the thousands of other words that you use day after day, if you will apply the memory techniques which follow.

The time to permanently learn how to spell a word is when you are in doubt about it and have to look it up in the dictionary. Spend a few moments to apply the methods of associating the correct spelling in your mind, and you will remember it whenever you need that word again.

Now let's see how easy it is to remember how to spell correctly. Listed are six secrets to spelling success. They are given below, with examples taken from a group of words that are considered "Spelling Demons."

Find the Trouble Area

First find the trouble area—the letter or letters in the word which cause you to spell the word incorrectly. Then you can proceed to apply one or more of the following hints.

Example: sep *A* rate. In the word "separate," the *A* is usually the trouble area.

I. Exaggerate the Trouble Area

Exaggerate the trouble area, then look away or close your eyes and visualize the word in its exaggerated form.

Example: sep **A** rate

II. Find a Word Within the Word

Find a word within the word that will include the area of difficulty.

Examples: *WE*ird
friEND
sac*RILE*gious

III. Develop a Linking Thought

Develop a linking thought to connect the trouble area of the word with the word itself.

Examples: A sac*ri*legious person *RILES* me. Stationery—A lett*er* is written on station*er*y.

IV. Break Into Syllables— Sound the Word

Notice how many words are pronounced exactly the way they are spelled.

Examples: ad / mit . . . ex / pel

V. Trace the Word

Feel the word by tracing it in the air or on paper with your finger. This paper could be a rough paper towel so that more feeling can be associated through the fingers. Then write the word as rapidly as you can—as you would write your own name.

VI. Apply Spelling Rules

Spelling rules were originally created to help individuals spell words correctly. If you remember a particular spelling rule and it can be applied to a word, then by all means do so.

Applying More Than One Method

In many instances, you will notice that you can apply more than one method to a given word. This additional method will strengthen the association for that particular word.

Example: DILEMMA

1. Exaggerate the trouble area—dile **MM** a.
2. Find a word within the word—dil*EMMA*.
3. Linking thought—*EMMA* is in a dil*EMMA*.
4. Sound the word and break into syllables—di / lem / ma.
5. Trace the word. Visualize it as you trace it.

Use Your Imagination

The next time you consult the dictionary for the correct spelling of a word, take a few extra moments to apply the methods you have learned. The following word that is graphically illustrated will stimulate your imagination and give you an idea of how the methods can be applied to a word. Attempt to make pictures of new words in your mind in a similar manner.

PARALLEL. *ALL* lines are par*ALL*el.

Spelling Demons

The following is a list of words frequently misspelled. These words can be learned and remembered permanently with the techniques you have been given. Have someone read this list of words to you and you spell them. When you find the words you now spell incorrectly, analyze each one and apply one or more of the methods you have learned. *Instructions:* First find the

Trouble Area, the letter or letters in the word that give you trouble. You can exaggerate them under the heading, "Trouble Area," or use one of the other methods given to find your link. You may find a word-within-the-word that contains the Trouble Area, or you may develop a linking thought association. Apply the method that works *best* for you.

WORD	TROUBLE AREA	ASSOCIATION
calendar	calend*A*r	*DA*ys are on a calen*DA*r.
weird	*WE*Ird	*WE* are never *WE*ird.
leisure	*LEI*sure	*IS* this le*IS*ure?
embarrassed	emba*RR*a*SS*ed	*R.R.* and *S*team*S*hip collide . . . emba*RR*a*SS*ed!
lieutenant	*LIE*utenant	*LIE–U–TEN–ANT*
villain		
occasion		
discipline		
guarantee		
committee		
irresistible		
supersede		
seize		
category		
descendant		
comparative		
bulletin		
tyranny		
anoint		
announce		
prefer		
excellent		
recommend		
secretary		
connoisseur		
balloon		

When you have written your associations for all of these words, cover the page and take a test of your retention.

ADDITIONAL PRACTICAL APPLICATION 229

Test Yourself

You should know how to correctly spell all the words on the preceding page. To check your progress take a test on the following words. Some words are spelled correctly, some are misspelled. Apply what you have learned, analyze, and write the word correctly in the space provided. For those words which you recognize as correctly spelled, put a check mark in the space for the correct spelling.

WORD	CORRECT SPELLING
comitee	committee
excellent	✓
garantee	guarantee
paralell	_____
comparative	_____
bulletin	_____
tyrany	_____
annoint	_____
prefere	_____
announce	_____
recommend	_____
secretery	_____
conoisseur	_____
balloon	_____
category	_____
descendent	_____
calendar	_____
wierd	_____
leisure	_____
embarassed	_____
lieutenant	_____
villian	_____
ocassion	_____
discipline	_____
irresistable	_____
superseed	_____
seize	_____

NUMBER SPELLED CORRECTLY _____

Continue to improve your spelling. Spelling correctly is extremely important in your everyday life, and proficiency will leave a good impression on the person you are corresponding with. When you are confronted with a word that you do not know how to spell correctly, spend a few moments *at that time* to associate the correct spelling of the word in your mind. Then when you need this word again, you will spell it correctly with confidence.

Remember Stock Symbols

Walking into a brokerage office can be a strange, mystifying experience unless you know in advance that stocks are usually traded by their symbols rather than by the corporation name. The stock symbol usually consists of a letter or letters found in the corporation name.

Oftentimes it is the first letter of each word found in the title or just the first letter of one of the words. You will find that most of the larger and older corporations use the first letter system, i.e., *G.M.* for General *Motors*, or *G.E.* for General *Electric*.

Other corporations have symbol letters found elsewhere in the name. For example: *IK* for *I*nterla*k*e Iron. Because there are literally thousands of corporations you will find an endless variety of symbols used. This even includes using the first letter of each word in the corporation name but in a reverse order.

One or more of these three rules should be applied to remember stock symbols:

1. INITIALS—*G.M.* = General *M*otors

2. EXAGGERATION through Imagination—Exaggerate the letter or letters in the symbol: J = Standard Oil of New **J**ersey.

3. LINKING THOUGHTS—Used when one of the symbol letters is not used in the corporation name: *X* = U.S. Steel. (Picture two U.S. Steel girders in the form of an "X," or think of U.*X*. Steel.)

Practice Exercise

The following is a list of 16 commonly traded stocks on the New York Stock Exchange. Study these symbols and in a few moments you can memorize the entire list of 16 stocks. You will be pleasantly surprised to find that the symbols fall easily into place. Any number of stock symbols can be memorized in this manner.

STOCK SYMBOL	COMPANY	ASSOCIATION
T	American **T**elephone & Telegraph	Exaggerate the *T*. Picture the huge *T* in Telephone.
GM	General *M*otors	Initial—*G.M.*
J	Standard Oil of New **J**ersey	Exaggerate the *J*. Picture the huge *J* in Jersey.
X	U.S. Steel (U.*X*. Steel)	Link—a steel *X*.
F	Ford	Initial—*F*.
LIT	**LIT** ton Industries	Exaggerate *LIT*. Also, the first three letters in LITTON.
GE	General *E*lectric	Initial—*G.E.*
HR	International **H** arveste **R**	Link—Have a *Happy Ride* on an *I-H* tractor.
IK	**I** nterla **K** e Iron	Link—*IK*e jumps *into the lake* holding an *iron*.
AV	**AV** co Corporation	Exaggerate. Also, first two letters in the name. *AV*
GO	Gulf *O*il	Initials—*G.O.* Link—*GO* with Gulf Oil.
TX	**T** e **X** aco	Exaggerate. Also man's name, *TeX*.
C	Chrsyler	Initial—*C*.
SWX	*SW*ift (*X*)	Link—*SW* in *SW*ift, and two pieces of bacon form an "*X*."
TWA	*T*rans *W*orld *A*irlines	Initials—*T.W.A.*
S	Sears Roebuck	Initial—*S*.

When you have associated these stocks and their symbols, turn the page and test your retention of abstract material.

Test Yourself

The following is the list of 16 stock symbols which you have just memorized. Write the name of the company represented by these symbols.

STOCK SYMBOL	COMPANY
GM	_____
J	_____
T	_____
X	_____
LIT	_____
F	_____
GE	_____
IK	_____
HR	_____
AV	_____
GO	_____
C	_____
TX	_____
SWX	_____
TWA	_____
S	_____

If you are interested in the stock market, take a list of 20 stocks and their symbols each day and memorize them. Within a short time you should have all the important symbols tied into your mind so that whenever you wish to recall them, they are at your fingertips.

Important Atomic Elements

An example of our memory training methods applied to remembering scientific facts is the following list of important atomic elements. The element is listed, along with its atomic number and atomic weight. A numerical word is formed to represent the atomic number and weight, then these two numerical words are associated to the element. Remember to use your imagination when associating these facts together.

Example: The Atomic Element Carbon. Carbon has the atomic number of 6 and atomic weight of 12.01. Visualize this Linking Thought. Take a sheet of CARBON paper and smear it on your JAW, then on your TIN SUIT.

ADDITIONAL PRACTICAL APPLICATION

When you wish to recall this information, think of CARBON and it should remind you of the carbon on your JAW, then your TIN SUIT. *JAW = 6*, the atomic number. *TIN SUIT = 12.01* the atomic weight

Two separate words were used to represent the weight because this tells you that the decimal point goes *between* the two words.

Make your own associations for the remainder of the list. The numerical words are already listed for you. When you have completed your associations, cover the page and test your retention. Remember that the one-word association represents the atomic number, and the two-word association represents the weight.

ELEMENT	NUMBER	ASSOCIATION FOR NUMBER	WEIGHT	ASSOCIATION FOR WEIGHT
Aluminum	13	*dome*	26.98	*niche–buff*
Arsenic	33	*memo*	74.91	*car–bed*
Barium	56	*lash*	137.36	*tomahawk–match*
Bismuth	83	*foam*	209.00	*inspect–sauce*
Boron	5	*oil*	10.82	*autos–fan*
Bromine	35	*mail*	79.916	*cup–potash*
Calcium	20	*nose*	40.08	*rose–sofa*
Carbon	6	*jaw*	12.01	*tin–suit*
Chlorine	17	*tag*	35.457	*mule–relic*
Chromium	24	*nero*	52.01	*lawn–seed*
Cobalt	27	*neck*	58.94	*love–bar*
Copper	29	*knob*	63.54	*chime–lair*
Fluorine	9	*ape*	19.00	*tub–seesaw*
Gold	79	*cap*	197.0	*tobacco–house*

When you have made all your associations, cover the page and take a test.

Test Yourself

Listed below are the atomic elements you have just memorized. First write in the words that you associated with that particular element, then translate these numerical words into the atomic number and atomic weight.

ELEMENT	ASSOCIATION FOR NUMBER	NUMBER	ASSOCIATION FOR WEIGHT	WEIGHT
Aluminum	_____	_____	_____	_____
Arsenic	_____	_____	_____	_____

ADDITIONAL PRACTICAL APPLICATION

ELEMENT	ASSOCIATION FOR NUMBER	NUMBER	ASSOCIATION FOR WEIGHT	WEIGHT
Barium				
Bismuth				
Boron				
Bromine				
Calcium				
Carbon				
Chlorine				
Chromium				
Cobalt				
Copper				
Fluorine				
Gold				

NUMBER CORRECT _____

You can associate the remaining Atomic Elements in the same manner. Notice, also, how you can easily remember the element symbol by recognizing that the initial system is applied in most instances. Usually it is the first two letters of the element itself.

Examples: Aluminum—Al. Barium—Ba.

Use your imagination for symbols that are not similar to the examples above.

GOLD—Au	The *AUTHOR* received a *GOLD* cup.
SILVER—Ag	*AGE* old *SILVER* coins.
POTASSIUM—K	Bang the *POT* and the *KETTLE* together.
TUNGSTEN—W	*WAGGING TONGUE*.
TIN—Sn	*TIN SNIPPERS*.

Be an Optimist!

The Optimist Creed truly expresses positive thinking. It says what we have been teaching throughout your memory training course. Keep a positive attitude and meet every memory challenge in a positive way. "SAY YES!"

Read the Optimist Creed three times from beginning to end, visualizing as you read. Then study the cues we have extracted from it. You can memorize the entire Optimist Creed with little effort by applying the principles of Cues and Linking Thoughts.

THE OPTIMIST CREED*

Promise Yourself—

To be so strong that nothing can disturb your peace of mind.
To talk health, happiness and prosperity to every person you meet.
To make all your friends feel that there is something in them.
To look at the sunny side of everything and make your optimism come true.
To think only of the best, to work only for the best and expect only the best.
To be just as enthusiastic about the success of others as you are about your own.
To forget the mistakes of the past and press on to the greater achievements of the future.
To wear a cheerful countenance at all times and give every living creature you meet a smile.
To give so much time to the improvement of yourself that you have no time to criticize others.
To be too large for worry, too noble for anger, too strong for fear, and too happy to permit the presence of trouble.

To memorize this material verbatim, work with it one line at a time. Extract the most meaningful cue or cues and write them beside the line. Try to pick cues that are as close as possible to the beginning of the line.

OPTIMIST CREED

Promise Yourself	(CUES)
To be so **strong** that nothing can disturb your peace of mind.	STRONG
To **talk h**ealth, **h**appiness and **p**rosperity to every person you meet.	TALK—H.H.P.
To make all your **friends** feel that there is something in them.	FRIENDS
To look at the **sunny side** of everything and make your optimism come true.	SUNNY SIDE

---
* Reprinted with permission of Optimist International.

To **think** only of the best, to **work** only for the best and **expect** only the best.	THINK, WORK, EXPECT
To be just as **enthusiastic** about the success of others as you are about your own.	ENTHUSIASTIC
To **forget** the mistakes of the **past** and press on to the greater achievements of the future.	FORGET PAST
To wear a **cheerful** countenance at all times and give every living creature you meet a smile.	CHEERFUL
To give so much time to the **improve**ment of yourself that you have no time to **criticize** others.	IMPROVE, CRITICIZE
To be too **large** for **worry**, too noble for **anger**, too strong for **fear**, and too happy to permit the presence of **trouble**.	LARGE, W A F T (**w**orry, **a**nger, **f**ear, **t**rouble)

You can memorize these cue words by associating them with your first 10 Visual Key Words. In the exercise that follows, we have given you the associations for the first five, then continue on your own and associate the remaining five in the same manner.

KEY WORD	EXTRACTED CUES	ASSOCIATION
1. HUT	strong	Visualize a *STRONG* hut.
2. HEN	Talk about H.H.P. *H*ealth, *H*appiness, *P*rosperity	See the hen *TALK H.H.P.*
3. HAM	friends	Picture your *FRIENDS* feeling that there is something in the ham.
4. HARE	sunny side	Picture the hare looking at the *SUNNY SIDE* of the street, and making his optimism come true.
5. HILL	think, work, expect	On top of the hill, see a statue of the *THINKER*, as he looks at the *WORKERS, EXPECTING* the best.

KEY WORD	EXTRACTED CUES	ASSOCIATION
6. JAY	enthusiastic	_____
7. HOOK	forget past	_____
8. HIVE	cheerful	_____
9. APE	improve, criticize	_____
10. TOES	large, WAFT	_____
	(*w*orry, *a*nger, *f*ear, *t*rouble)	

Now that you have associated all these cue words in your mind, cover the page and take a test of your retention.

Test Yourself

Here are your Visual Key Words from 1–10. Think of your Key Word and you should recall the cue word which was extracted from the Optimist Creed.

VISUAL KEY WORD	CUES
1. HUT	_____
2. HEN	_____
3. HAM	_____
4. HARE	_____
5. HILL	_____
6. JAY	_____
7. HOOK	_____
8. HIVE	_____
9. APE	_____
10. TOES	_____

NUMBER CORRECT _____

Memorize the Cues in Sequence

There is still another method that can be applied to remember these cues extracted from the Optimist Creed. This method is Linking Thoughts, where you memorize the cues by making a story from them, visualizing the progression of the story from one cue to the next.

CUES	LINKING THOUGHTS
STRONG	
TALK _____	to your
FRIENDS _____	and they will look on the
SUNNY SIDE _____	of life for the
T. W. E. BEST _____	and be
ENTHUSIASTIC, _____	also never
FORGET _____	to be
CHEERFUL _____	at all
TIMES _____	while riding on a
LARGE WAFT.	

Write It Verbatim

You have memorized the cues which were extracted from the Optimist Creed. Go back to the beginning and read the Optimist Creed once again from beginning to the end. Visualize as you read and recognize how the cues will help you to keep the sequence in mind. Then attempt to write the Optimist Creed verbatim on the lines provided below.

_____
_____
_____
_____
_____
_____
_____
_____
_____
_____
_____
_____

Compare your written version with the original Optimist Creed. If you find that you left out any words, then read it again, emphasizing the words that you omitted. And remember to be an optimist!

Verbatim Learning Techniques

1. Read three times from beginning to end for whole idea.
2. Visualize as you read.
3. Extract cues and notice relationships.
4. Memorize cues, using Linking Thought method.
5. Re-read for whole idea.
6. Try reciting verbatim.
7. Review within 24 hours. Use as soon as possible.

Congratulations!

You are now ready for your post-graduate course in memory training.

Your future classroom will be your daily environment; the textbooks will be the people and facts you remember. The added success and pleasure in your business and social life will be your reward.

Although this memory training course is now completed, you are just beginning to work with memory techniques. You will find it fun and stimulating to daily apply these newly learned methods to everything around you. Faithful application will stimulate your powers of concentration. Your observation and visualization will remain awake and sharp.

Imagine this analogy: "Your memory is similar to a muscle in that it strengthens with use, weakens with disuse."

Keep a positive, confident attitude and you will be continually rewarded with a MEMORY FOR FUN AND PROFIT.

Yours for a most retentive memory,

ARTHUR BORNSTEIN
Los Angeles, California